Beyond Morning Message

Dozens of Dazzling Ideas for Interactive Letters to the Class
That Enhance Shared Reading, Writing, Math, and More!

BY VALERIE SCHIFFERDANOFF

SCHOLASTIC
PROFESSIONAL BOOKS

NEW YORK • TORONTO • LONDON • AUCKLAND • SYDNEY
MEXICO CITY • NEW DELHI • HONG KONG

Dedicated to my mother,

Gertrude Goldsholl Schiffer,

who cherished and saved every letter

my sisters and I ever wrote.

ACKNOWLEDGMENT

Joanna Davis-Swing, editor. Well done!

Front cover and interior design by Kathy Massaro
Cover photograph by Richard Hutchings
Photographs on pages 5, 18, 29, 36, 61, 71, and 84 by Richard Hutchings.
Illustrations on page 8 by Maxie Chamblis
All others courtesy of author.

ISBN 0-439-11108-0
Copyright © 2001 by Valerie SchifferDanoff
All rights reserved.
Printed in the USA

CONTENTS

Dear Reader,

For the past ten years, Daily Letters have been an integral part of my day. In kindergarten, first-, and second-grade classrooms, the Daily Letter has become an invaluable teaching tool that lets me model reading and writing every day. At the same time, I can focus on specific literacy and content-area knowledge and skills. The predictable format gives my young students the structure they need, and the flexibility lets me tailor my teaching for each class. When I realized all the teaching and learning opportunities the Daily Letter offers—extending far beyond the traditional morning message—I wanted to share my ideas with other teachers.

I begin the very first day of school with a Daily Letter. I set it on my easel directly in front of our meeting area, where children can gather comfortably. After students have stored their bags in their cubbies, placed their folders on their seats, signed up for lunch, and greeted their friends, they gather in front of the Daily Letter for the next part of their morning routine. I often find children congregating in front of the Daily Letter even before their bags are put away. They miss the letter when I am absent or cannot write one due to special scheduling. It is a welcoming fixture of our classroom.

On the first day of school, when second-graders see a letter written especially for them, they might say:

> Look at those strange words!
> I love that sticker!
> That face looks like me!
> Oh, is that how you spell September?!

Seeing all that excitement, I can not help but respond with,

> Well let's sit down in front of the letter and see what it has to say!

You may be thinking: "I'm not sure I could write a letter every day." Read on! It's easier than you think and well worth the effort. When you see how much children enjoy it, how well it integrates all sorts of learning, and how easily it builds a sense of community, composing the letter will become a seamless part of your teaching. Think of it as writing to a friend or a whole class of friends; the words will flow naturally.

To help you on your way, I've compiled this collection of sample letters, lessons, and teaching ideas. As you read, select and adapt those that will work for you and your children. Let the learning begin!

Valerie SchifferDanoff

The Basics
of a Daily Letter

A Daily Letter is a teacher-written text that can be a springboard to reading, writing, spelling, vocabulary, math, and content-area activities. It serves as a model for writing every day and helps foster a sense of community in your classroom. As you write to your students about classroom activities, the weather, the weekend, upcoming events, and other things on your mind, you can easily weave in literacy concepts and content-area knowledge, all while making your students feel special and important. Students will enthusiastically approach the familiar page that greets them every morning (or after lunch, or any other time that suits your schedule) and eagerly work through it. Keeping the format friendly is the key to engaging and sustaining student interest, and this chapter provides plenty of ideas for making the letter appealing to students. Subsequent chapters provide a wealth of rich teaching possibilities using the Daily Letter.

Second graders enjoy reading their letter and filling in the blanks.

What You Need to Write a Daily Letter

I prefer to write the letter on 1-inch-lined chart paper, which helps me stay neat so it's easy to read. For younger students it's helpful to skip lines. Since I send the letter home with the class helper, I use chart paper that's perforated on top.

I am most comfortable writing the letter in the morning before school begins. This way I am fresh and can include such things as weather conditions, daily reminders, homework recaps, previous-day experiences, changes in the daily routine, and spontaneous events. You can write it the night before (if you're not a morning person!). In a pinch you can prepare letters a few days ahead, although letters lose their immediacy that way.

To prepare your letter, you need the following items:

- ✳ chart paper
- ✳ markers
- ✳ stickers
- ✳ clip art

- ✳ sticky notes
- ✳ correction fluid (in case you make a mistake while writing)

To present your letter, it's helpful to have the following items on hand:

- ✳ chart stand or table easel
- ✳ easel clips

- ✳ highlighting markers
- ✳ highlighting tape

Making the Daily Letter Kid-Pleasing

Here are some easy ways to spice up your letters:

✳ Use a rebus style by drawing simple pictures, such as

- faces above "boys" and "girls."
- a sun.
- clouds around the words describing cloudy weather.
- eyeballs above "see" or "look."
- a shape when writing about shapes.

✳ Use stickers for rebus.

✳ Use clip art by tracing or gluing for rebus.

✳ Use stamps for rebus.

✳ Draw speech balloons. You can even buy these as stickers.

To get you started, I have provided some traceable rebus symbols on page 8. You can trace them through chart paper directly onto your letter.

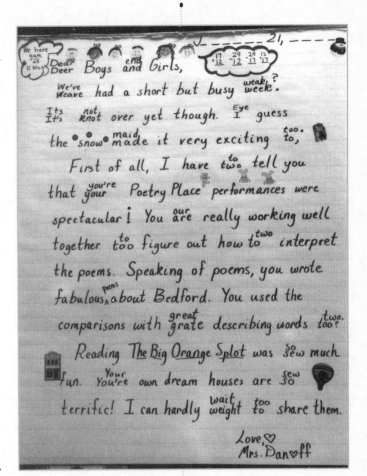

If the letter is neat, colorful, and attractive, students will flock to it naturally.

Daily Letters in Kindergarten

Reading and writing are new and exciting endeavors for kindergartners. For many children, your classroom may be their first experience with written communication. Letter writing can show children how personal this form of communication can be.

The Daily Letter lets kindergartners explore written language. As you read it aloud and point to the words, they learn that print carries meaning and can express personal thoughts and feelings. You model left-to-right, top-to-bottom, and return-sweep directional movements. You reinforce one-to-one word matching and demonstrate how to use picture clues. Over time, students will be able to locate known and unknown words, recognize the difference between a letter and a word, and identify beginning and ending sounds. While you may be encouraging temporary spelling in student work, your letter models correct spelling every day. All this modeling helps your students develop early reading behaviors.

(Continued on page 9)

Reproducible Rebus Symbols

Beyond Morning Message

Scholastic Professional Books

Tips for Writing to Kindergartners

Keep the following ideas in mind when writing to kindergartners:

* Form large letters, using two lines on lined chart paper, so children can easily see each letter's shape.

* Write with brightly-colored markers, not pastels.

* Limit the length of the letter to three or four simple sentences.

* Write each sentence in a different color.

* Repeat some words and sentences every day to build familiarity.

* Use a rebus style as much as possible. (See rebus ideas.)

* Keep the language simple and natural (e.g., *Today is Tuesday. We have music.*).

Teaching Kindergartners with Daily Letters

If you're excited about the letter, your enthusiasm will captivate your students and motivate them to read it. Here are some tips for helping your learners interact with—and make sense of—a Daily Letter:

* Give students an opportunity to look at the letter independently before you read it aloud.

* Ask them to describe what they see (i.e., words, letters, pictures, patterns).

* Ask them if they see something in today's letter that is the same as or different from yesterday's letter.

* Using a pointer, point to each word as you read the letter sentence by sentence to the class. This practice helps children track from left to right.

* Pace yourself and stop between sentences to ask questions about what you've read, reinforcing the idea that reading is making meaning out of symbols.

* Give children opportunities to come up to the letter and touch or point to words, letters, and pictures.

* Gently guide the child's hand to the correct place if necessary.

As children become familiar with the letter and its format, leave blank spaces for individual letters and invite children to come up and fill them in. If a child writes a letter incorrectly, congratulate the effort. Ask if she can be your puppet and allow you to move her hand to write the letter correctly. Eventually, children may be able to fill in entire words.

As the year progresses more time can be spent on the letter. The activity can go from ten minutes to as long as thirty-five minutes, depending on content and what is being highlighted.

Literacy-Building Activities for Kindergarten

I've discovered many, many ways to teach kindergartners with Daily Letters. Below is a compilation of my ideas to get you started. You'll surely discover new twists as you go along. As your children gain literacy skills, be sure to check out the list for first grade on page 12, too.

ACTIVITY	USE FOR:
Clap words.	☀ enhancing auditory discrimination ☀ teaching syllables
Invite children to circle specific letters or words with a highlighter.	☀ building letter/word recognition ☀ working on initial and final consonant sounds and medial vowels
Ask children to circle all the words that begin or end with a particular letter.	☀ building letter recognition ☀ developing letter-sound associations
Write one letter in the same color throughout the message.	☀ building letter recognition
Cover up initial consonant sound with a sticky note.	☀ working on beginning letter sounds
Challenge students to match a letter or word written on a sticky note to a letter or word in the Daily Letter.	☀ building letter and word recognition
Encourage students to cup their hands around words to help them recognize and identify sounds and letters.	☀ building letter-sound associations
Omit a letter from a word, leaving a blank space to indicate where it should go. Invite children to write in the missing letter.	☀ practicing forming letters ☀ building letter-sound associations
Choose a word like *cat*; ask children to think of words that rhyme with it.	☀ introducing word families, spelling patterns, rhyme
Ask children to identify individual words.	☀ building sight word vocabulary
Model the handwriting "letter of the day" by using it in the letter.	☀ developing handwriting skills

For kindergartners the Daily Letter helps develop phonemic awareness, visual discrimination, early reading behaviors, and writing skills, and encourages children to expand their attention span and take risks.

Daily Letters in First Grade

This is the year many children become readers. Most are ready and anxious to get started, yet they still need to be encouraged to take risks and practice their reading and writing skills.

Tips for Writing to First Graders

Capitalize on your students' eagerness to read by making the Daily Letter an important part of their day. Here are some strategies for ensuring that the Daily Letter is appealing to all of your budding readers:

When creating the letter:

* use brightly colored markers, not pastels.

* write 7–9 sentences.

* skip lines and use a whole line space to form letters.

* write each sentence in a different color.

* begin with simple language. As the year progresses, incorporate adjectives, adverbs, and more challenging vocabulary.

* follow a friendly letter format; including the date and a P.S. is okay too.

* repeat selected text each day, such as "Today is our _____ day of school. It is Monday."

* use a rebus style as much as possible, especially at the beginning of the year.

* avoid making predictions, like "We will go outside for recess today." You can avoid some big disappointments this way!

When using the letter:

* begin by asking children what they see now that is the same as or different from the previous day's letter.

* invite children to read independently to themselves or look for words they know. Before reading with the whole class, ask children to come up and identify words they know.

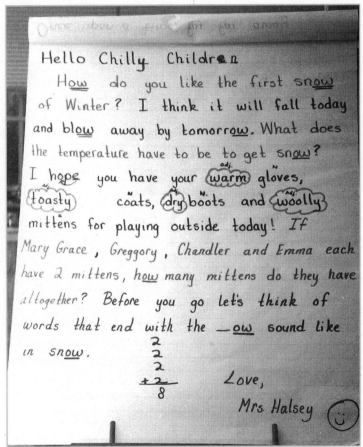

This first-grade letter capitalizes on the excitement of the winter's first snow. Notice that Mrs. Halsey omitted ending sounds so she could focus on the -ow sound.

✴ use a pointer as you read chorally with the whole class. As the year progresses (usually around November), ask if anyone would like to read a whole sentence aloud to the class.

Literacy-Building Activities for First Grade

The possibilities for teaching with a Daily Letter in first grade include all the kindergarten ideas on page 10 as well as those on the following list:

ACTIVITY	USE FOR:
Count and circle sentences with highlighters.	✴ reinforcing idea of sentence ✴ highlighting punctuation
Omit letters for children to fill in, leaving one space per missing letter.	✴ working with consonant clusters, vowels, digraphs, or any letter you want to focus on
Write prefixes or suffixes in a different color.	✴ focusing on word parts
Cover up words or parts of words with sticky notes.	✴ working on syllabification, word chunks, or other decoding skills
Write different consonants on sticky notes and invite children to place them over a written word, creating a new word.	✴ exploring word families and spelling patterns
Invite children to brainstorm words that rhyme with a word used in the letter.	✴ exploring word families and spelling patterns
Highlight compound words.	✴ introducing and exploring compound words
Include word choices that are homonyms, such as *The sun/son is out today.*	✴ discussing and practicing homonyms
Include word choices that are synonyms. Invite students to choose the one they like best.	✴ choosing the right word
Include a simile.	✴ introducing and exploring similes
Incorporate a familiar poem. Omit some words and challenge the children to think of replacements.	✴ exploring poetry ✴ choosing appropriate words ✴ finding rhyming words

First graders often become independent readers by spring, so come April, you may find them congregating around the letter each morning before you have a chance to get there. They may also have their own ideas about how to use the letter. Encourage their input, and make an effort to try out their suggestions. For instance, one of my classes asked if they could pick the next person to come up to the letter. That began "Pick a Friend Friday," which became a class favorite.

Extended Teaching with the Daily Letter

❉ During small-group guided reading, ask children to find words from the story they've just read in the Daily Letter.

❉ For emergent readers, reread the letter in a small group to develop word recognition and fluency.

❉ Encourage children to use the letter as a model for correct spelling and organization of ideas.

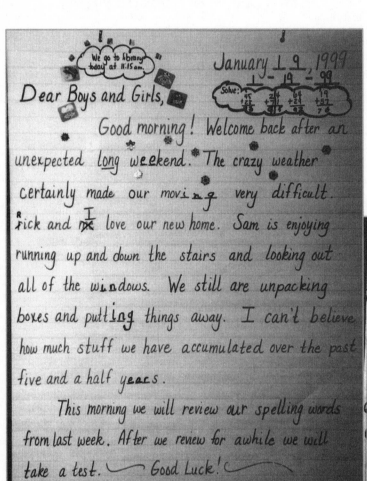

This first-grade letter focused on the -ing ending and middle vowel sounds.

This letter enabled students to practice telling time, counting, and forming the past tense of verbs.

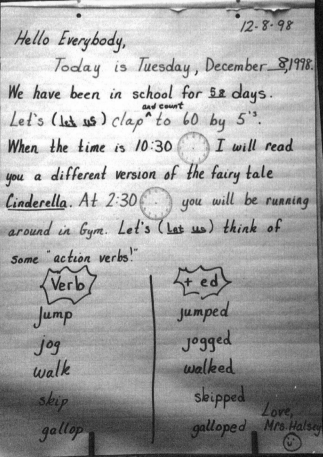

Daily Letters in Second Grade

Second graders quickly discover they can actually read the letter. The excitement and confidence this realization sparks makes it worthwhile to begin the year with a simple letter that all students can read with little difficulty. Of course, you probably have a few students still working on pulling the reading process together; the Daily Letter affords them an excellent opportunity to practice the skills and strategies they need.

Tips for Writing to Second Graders

Although second graders are often experienced readers, it's still important to entice them into the text by making the letter visually appealing. Here are some specific tips:

When creating the letter:

* skip lines, and use a whole line space to form letters. For longer letters, continue onto a second page or onto the back and use an easel clip to hold the letter in place.

* use single lines when including poems or story excerpts.

* use brightly colored markers, not pastels.

* write 7–12 varied and descriptive sentences.

* write each sentence in a different color; this may only be necessary early in the school year.

* use rebus for fun and for word sounds—like a key for "tur-key."

* follow a friendly letter format; including the date and a P. S. is okay.

* avoid making predictions about possible early dismissal for snowstorms and other potential events, since second graders can be just as easily disappointed as anyone else.

Literacy-Building Activities for Second Grade and Beyond

In addition to the ideas for first grade presented on page 12, you can try the following activities to teach and reinforce reading skills:

ACTIVITY	USE FOR:
Invite children to read entire letter independently to themselves. Ask for volunteers to read sentences aloud.	✳ building fluency
Review reading-response skills.	✳ building comprehension
Incorporate spelling words into the letter.	✳ reviewing spelling words
Stop in the middle of the letter and ask a comprehension question.	✳ building comprehension skills; modeling reading strategies
Omit letters in words, leaving one blank space for each missing letter.	✳ focusing on vowel sounds, digraphs, consonant blends, or spelling patterns
Ask students to clap words.	✳ building syllabication and dictionary skills (students check answers in the dictionary)
Circle punctuation with highlighter.	✳ introducing and reviewing punctuation marks
Invite students to think of words that rhyme with a word used in the letter. Write these on a separate rhyming word chart.	✳ exploring word families
Offer a choice of two antonyms for a word in a sentence. Have students choose one and explain their choice.	✳ checking comprehension
Write homonyms for a word in the letter and challenge students to choose the correct one.	✳ practicing spelling
Circle several words and invite students to generate synonyms (or antonyms) for each word. Write substitutions above the original word.	✳ exploring word choice ✳ expanding vocabulary
Write synonyms for several words on sticky notes and post them on the side of the letter. Ask children to put a sticky note over its synonym in the letter.	✳ expanding vocabulary
Circle verbs, nouns, and adjectives with different-colored markers.	✳ introducing/reviewing parts of speech
Circle suffixes and root words.	✳ exploring word parts
Write down what children are saying as they enter the room, using quotation marks around their words.	✳ teaching dialogue and quotation marks
Identify contractions. Write the contracted words above contraction.	✳ teaching contractions

Second-Grade Letters

We worked on antonyms and homonyms this chilly morning.

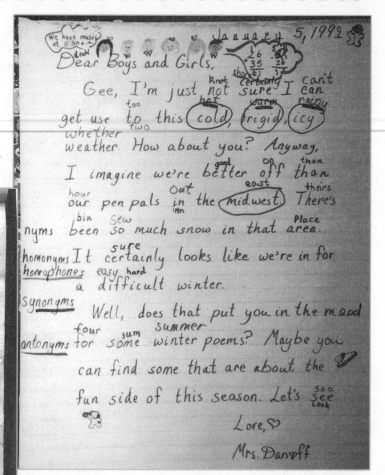

January 5, 1992

Dear Boys and Girls,

Gee, I'm just not sure I can get use to this (cold, frigid, icy) weather. How about you? Anyway, I imagine we're better off than our pen pals in the (midwest) There's been so much snow in that area. It certainly looks like we're in for a difficult winter.

Well, does that put you in the mood for some winter poems? Maybe you can find some that are about the fun side of this season. Let's see.

Love,
Mrs. Danoff

margin annotations: knot, certainly, cant, too, hot, warm, racey, whether, two, good, on, then, hour, Out, east, theirs, bin, sew, Place, nyms, homonyms, homophones, sure, easy, hard, synonyms, antonyms, four, sum, summer, sea, see, look

---

May 20, 1999

Dear Three times Six plus One times Two Children,

$3 \times 6 = 18 + 1 \times 2 = 2 = 20$

You know whenever I read about Elmer with a class, it's always wonderful. We also try to really figure out just how many tangerines Elmer eats. I think we can all agree that he begins by picking thirty-one. Then he does eat seven right away. Next he replaces those seven by picking seven more. Once he arrives at Wild Island he wants to eat twelve, but he only eats three. That's really where we're up to now. So let's see what happens in the next chapters.

Love,
Mrs. Danoff

margin annotations: 18÷6=3, 18, 6|18, 3|18, ure, doze, treasure, sure, figure, measure, pressure, pleasure, tissue, capture, lecture, leisure, texture, mixture, Miniature, picture

My second graders worked on rhyming words this day; notice the list they brainstormed on the left side of the page.

By circling nouns, verbs, and adjectives in different colors, we worked on parts of speech.

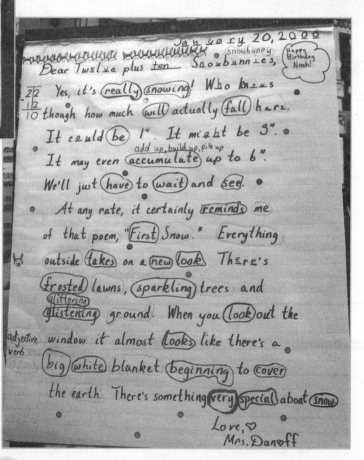

January 20, 2000

Dear Twelve plus ten Snowbunnies,

Yes, it's (really) (snowing)! Who knows though how much (will) actually (fall) here. It could (be) 1". It might be 3". It may even (accumulate) up to 6". We'll just (have) to (wait) and (see). At any rate, it certainly (reminds) me of that poem, "(First) Snow." Everything outside (takes) on a (new) (look). There's (frosted) lawns, (sparkling) trees and (glittering) (glistening) ground. When you (look) out the window it almost (looks) like there's a (big) (white) blanket (beginning) to (cover) the earth. There's something (very) (special) about (snow)

Love,
Mrs. Danoff

margin annotations: 2½, -1½, 10, snowbunny, Happy Birthday Noah!, add up, build up, pile up, adjective, verb

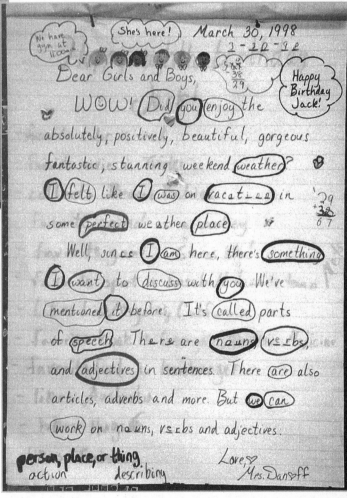

I focused on contractions and word endings in this letter.

We talked about and circled various parts of speech after reading this letter.

While reading the next few chapters, remember to give yourself time to experiment with Daily Letter writing. Write some at home, first. Then, copy them onto chart paper. You'll soon develop your own style and routine, and you'll discover the best way to make the Daily Letter a valuable part of your day.

Introducing the Daily Letter to Your Class

The Daily Letter is an excellent way to kick off a new school year. It provides a predictable routine that remains through the whole year and focuses and motivates students. Beginning with a Daily Letter also gives you the opportunity to informally assess your class as a whole on the very first day, and to continue this assessment throughout the year.

If the first day of school has come and gone without a Daily Letter, you can easily incorporate it into your routine. Simply choose a regular time you'd like to gather your children for literacy-building activities and write a note to your students. They will love the personal format and engaging activities—no matter when in the school year you introduce it—and you will love the flexibility and adaptability this teaching tool allows.

No matter when you first introduce the Daily Letter, you'll want to be full of enthusiasm to capture your students' attention. Making the letter attractive (see page 7) and the content appealing to your learners will ensure success. The scenarios in this chapter provide ideas for introducing the Daily Letter in kindergarten through grade 2 classrooms.

Kicking Off a New Year in Kindergarten

Kindergartners are eager learners and are thrilled to see a letter just for them waiting on the easel. Since they may not have much experience reading and writing, keep the first letter short and simple, and include the names of all your pupils because some may be able to recognize their names. Also, establish a consistent format so students will begin to recognize words and patterns that are repeated every day.

At right is a sample first-day letter to a kindergarten class. The salutation, first line, and closing can remain the same throughout the year, while the date and second line will change slightly each day. This predictability will build confidence in your young readers. Below is a transcription of how I introduced a similar letter to a kindergarten class.

September 7, 1999

Dear Boys and Girls,

Good morning!
1
Today is our first day of school.
⌢⌢
I am so happy to see Sara, John, Enid, Pete, (etc.)

We can play and have fun.

Love,
Mrs. Danoff

Mrs. Danoff:	Our class is so special! I am going to write you a letter every day. Have you or your parents ever received a letter in the mail?
Enid:	Sometimes I look in the mail box with my mommy. But only she can take the letters out.
Pete:	I got your letter last week.
Kendra:	Me, too!
Mrs. Danoff:	Well, guess what! A letter will be here every day, just like it is today, waiting for you. Every day, we can read the letter together and at the end of the day, our special helper will get to take the letter home to keep.
Sara:	Can we read it now?
Luis:	Yes, can we? I think I see my name!
Mrs. Danoff:	Yes, you're right. Luis, come up and point to your name. Let's read the rest of the letter now and find everyone's name.

For kindergartners on their first day, it's best to keep the dialogue fairly simple and short.

Extension Activities

Here are some simple extension activities you can use with a letter similar to the one described above:

✳ Write student names in dotted lines that they can trace over.

✳ Give children a letter on a piece of a sentence strip and ask them to find words that begin or end with that letter.

Follow-up

The next day, keep a few elements the same (e.g., salutation, first line, closing), and add some new text that reflects what's going on that day. You can change the "I am so happy to see…" sentence to "It is Wednesday." The next sentence can be "I can see the sun (or clouds)." Look at all the teaching you can do from this one letter.

September 8, 1999

Dear Boys and Girls,

Good morning!

2
Today is our second day of school.

It is Wednesday.

I can see the sun.

We can play and have fun.

Love,
Mrs. Danoff

2
second

Working on cardinal and ordinal numbers begins. Write the numeral 2 above the word *second*.

Wednesday

Working on days of the week begins.

---

sun

Working on weather words begins.

Good morning!   We can play and have fun.

Repeat phrases to begin word recognition.

My presentation went something like this:

Mrs. Danoff: Let's all look at the letter today. Who can tell me something they see that is the same as in the letter from yesterday?

Maria: I think I see your name.

Lee: *Love.*

Jose: I see a big *G.*

Enid: I remember those two eyeballs above that word.

Danny: That word is *see*!

Mrs. Danoff: Good for you! Now tell me something different that you see.

Jose: Well you didn't draw that sun yesterday.

Mrs. Danoff: That's right! Why do you think I drew a sun over that word?

Maggie: It's sunny today!

Mrs. Danoff: Very good! That word says *sun*, s-u-n, *sun*. Sun begins with the letter *s*. Can you find another word that begins with the letter *s* in this letter? Raise your hand, and when I call on you, you can come up to the letter and point to the *s*.

[Alternatively, you may have a child circle the letter with a marker, or write the letter on a sticky note and invite a student to come up and match it to an s in the letter.]

Maria: How come my name isn't in the letter today?

Mrs. Danoff: Some of the words in the letter are the same as yesterday, but some of the words are different. Can you tell me something else that is different today from yesterday?

Jose: Well, I know yesterday was the first day of school and you wrote a 1. Today you wrote a 2.

If there are particular letters and letter sounds you want to work on, changing one sentence in the letter can easily change the lesson. For instance, "I can see the sun" can be changed to "I have an apple for a snack," followed by "Do you have an apple too?" The children might then notice the word or picture of an apple. The dialogue would shift to a discussion of the letter *a*. It's easy to make the letter fit your instructional focus.

Mrs. Cacciapaglia welcomed her kindergartners with this bright and inviting letter.

September 7, 1999

Dear Boys and Girls,

Good morning! Today is our **1** first day of school. It's terrific Tuesday! I can see you are all ready for a new school year. I am too.

We have 21 children in our class. They are Sally, John, Sara, Ulysses, Michael, Enid, Jeffrey, Josh, Angel, Alec, Tiffany, Julie, Peter, Zachary, Marie, Donald, Chris, Hannah, Cody, Brittany and Benny.

There are a lot of fun things to do in first grade. Can you tell me something you want to learn to do?

We have so much to do today. So let's get busy!

Love,
Mrs. Danoff

P.S. It is still summer until September 21, 1999

Kicking Off a New Year in First Grade

First graders are typically more familiar with print than kindergartners, so their first letter may be longer. However, the same general principles about repetition and familiarity apply, especially in the beginning of the year. As their reading ability develops, you will have more flexibility in what you write.

At left is a sample first-grade letter.

| **1** first | Begin working on cardinal and ordinal numbers. |

| terrific Tuesday | Begin working on alliteration and days of the week. |

| Can you tell me something you want to learn to do? | Set up rules for raising hands. Then, use a questions like this as a great way to get a class discussion going. |

| P.S. It is still summer until September 21, 1999 | Introduce science and weather right away. Ask if anyone knows why it is still summer even though they are in school. |

Here's how I introduced this letter to first graders:
"I just love checking my mail each day. Sometimes there's a letter from a friend. You and your family may receive cards or letters, too. Well, I write a letter to the class each day. Each day one of you will get to take it home. This year you can learn how to write letters too."

Then I invite children to look at the letter and describe what they see. They point out familiar words, bright colors, and fun stickers. The activity gets started almost by itself, and may sound something like this:

Mrs. Danoff: Tell me what you see.
Zach: Pictures!
Donald: Words!
Hannah: Sentences!
Peter: My name and Benny's name, too!
Mrs. Danoff: Great!
Josh: I see *Boys*.
Julie: And I see *Girls*.
Sally: That's a pretty yellow.

Pacing is important. You want to encourage everyone who notices something to contribute, but be ready to move on if the responses become repetitive, if the chatter loses its focus, or if the room falls silent. Continue the activity by using a pointer to read the letter to and with the class, stopping along the way to discuss the content. Your conversation may go like this:

Mrs. Danoff: [After reading, "We have 21 children in our class."] Let's see now. Is everyone here today? How can we find out?
Enid: By counting!
Mrs. Danoff: What a good idea! Let's do that. [Counts students.] Well, now that we know everyone is here, let's all continue reading together. [Reads names.] Yes, that's everyone. Raise your hand if your name begins with an *A*.
Zachary: What if you have an *a* in your name?
Mrs. Danoff: Today we're just focusing on the first letter of your name.
[We continue through the alphabet, and then read the rest of the letter.]
Mrs. Danoff: Who can tell me why I wrote, "It is still summer until September 21, 1999"?
Sally: Because it's still warm.
Hannah: Because then it becomes winter.
Mrs. Danoff: Well, on September 21 it will become another season. But that's not winter. Does anyone know what season is after summer?
Angel: Oh, I think it's fall 'cause the leaves fall off then.
Mrs. Danoff: Good for you! That's right. So, even though our summer vacation is over, the season has not changed. That's why it is still warm outside. I really love the warm weather. How about the rest of you. Do you like summer best?

First graders quickly learn to chime in on "Good morning!" "Today is our ___ day of school," "So let's get busy!" and "Love, Mrs. Danoff." Those are the repeat phrases they see every day. The changing sentences become more and more readable as the year progresses. However, you can assess daily, as you listen and watch, to see who is reading which words.

What a Reader!

What can you do if someone says, "I can read the whole letter!" Congratulate that child. Then say he or she can help you read the letter to the class every day. You may want to say that he or she is ready to work on spelling. Fluent readers are not necessarily the best spellers. Once you begin omitting letters for cloze and phonics instruction, that child may face more of a challenge.

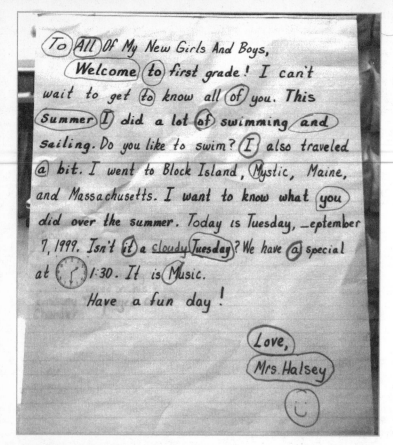

To All Of My New Girls And Boys,
Welcome to first grade! I can't wait to get to know all of you. This Summer I did a lot of swimming and sailing. Do you like to swim? I also traveled a bit. I went to Block Island, Mystic, Maine, and Massachusetts. I want to know what you did over the summer. Today is Tuesday, _eptember 7, 1999. Isn't it a cloudy Tuesday? We have a special at 1:30. It is Music.
Have a fun day!
Love,
Mrs. Halsey

▲ Mrs. Halsey got right to work on the first day of first grade.

Extension Activities

Some activities you can try on the first day in first grade include the following:

✳ Give children pieces of sentence strips or sticky paper on which to write their names or the first letter of their names. Challenge the children to match the strip to or place the sticky paper near their name as it appears in the letter. Though this may be easy for some, it won't be for everyone. A quick look will tell you who is using just the first letter to identify their name. One object of this activity is to make children more comfortable with coming up to the letter and taking a risk. Childen may trade strips with a friend and try to find the friend's name. For those children having difficulty with placement, gently guide their hands to the right place.

✳ Following this activity, you may want to have children line up in alphabetical order or have them locate their seats by matching their sticky notes or sentence strips correctly with their labeled desk. This can lead the children to sit down and be ready for the next activity.

✳ For a creative activity, ask children to draw a picture of their favorite summer activity. This can then lead to a sharing discussion.

September 7, 1999
Dear girls and _oys,
Welcome to _irst grade. I am very _appy that we will be learning and working together. We will go to _usic today.
Sincerely,
Mrs. Ertischek

◀ Mrs. Ertischek's simple, inviting letter sets the stage for a year of learning.

Kicking Off a New Year in Second Grade

Second graders are more sophisticated readers, so your first letter can have a little more pizzazz—but keep in mind that they've just returned from a three-month vacation and possibly a three-month hiatus from reading!

This past school year began on a Tuesday, which I designated as "Tangled Tuesday." Here's the letter that greeted my class that first day. As you can see, I scrambled all the students' names—"tangled" them. Since second graders usually rush to read the letter themselves, I challenged them to find their own and their classmates' names in the letter. With 22 students, it took about ten minutes for this activity, which allowed everyone to get settled and join in.

To help kids out (it was, after all, the first day of school!), I referred them to the pocket chart on the bulletin board that welcomed the class—and had everyone's name written correctly. Our discussion went something like this:

> We have art today at 11.15 a.m.
>
> September 7, 1999
> Welcome Back!
>
> Dear Boys and Girls,
> Today is not just our first day of school. It's also tangled Tuesday.
> Can you guess why?
> Well just look at who's in our class. There's yilen, suryc, homats, vane, stainu, yentrouc, enadeleli, laxdanred, regoryg, cajuiq, larcy, naene, anksjoc, hoah, celhra, ristianhc, ralua, thabeliza, neirtakhe, noails, einpahteps and reandz and hatmos.
> I wonder, what do you all know about second grade? What would you like to know about second grade? What would you like to learn in second grade?
> Love
> Mrs. Danoff

I scrambled the names of my 22 students for some first-day fun.

Jacqui:	Wow! There are some strange words there!
Mrs. Danoff:	Yes! Can you read the first sentence of this letter? It may help you figure out the words.
Thomas:	[After reading] It says this is Tangled Tuesday. What does that mean?
Mrs. Danoff:	Well, can anybody tell me what *tangled* means?
Laura:	My mom says my hair gets tangled.
Evan:	Sometimes my fishing line gets tangled.
Gregory:	My shoelaces get that way too.
Mrs. Danoff:	So, when something is tangled, what do you have to do?
Thomas:	Untangle it!
Jacqui:	Straighten it out!
Mrs. Danoff:	Do you think those strange words are tangled? What does the sentence before the tangled words say?

Jacqui:	[After reading] It talks about who is in our class.
Mrs. Danoff:	Yes, and I've tangled all your names. Let's continue reading the letter. We'll have to use phonics to sound out these "tangled names." See if you can each find your own name. Then you can help a friend too.

As children try to find their names, they may need some encouragement.

Laura:	[As she sounds out words] That sounds funny.
Rachel:	I think that's my name; it has most of the letters.
Mrs. Danoff:	Well let's see, Rachel. Does it have an *r, a, c, h, e, l*?
Rachel:	Yes! Hmm, then I guess it is my name. It just looks and sounds so funny as *celhra*!
Evan:	I found my name! Gee, that's like a weather vane instead of Evan.

Once everyone found their name, I invited each one to come up and write the correct name above the tangled word. Then we continued reading the letter.

In second grade, I begin by telling the class that the letter is my journal, and that I will write a journal entry and share it with them every day. Journal writing is a key part of my second-grade writing program, and the Daily Letter serves as an excellent model for students. I refer to it often as such throughout the year.

I wonder, what do you all know about second grade?	What would you like to know about second grade?

What would you like to learn in second grade?

Responding to these three sentences is our first journal entry and shared writing. For this first-day lesson, I may say something like this:

Mrs. Danoff:	How many of you have seen your teacher write a letter before? Does mine look the same or different? It's different because, for one thing, I am a different person. Each person's is different because writing is very personal.

After we have read the questions in the second paragraph:

Mrs. Danoff:	Well, who can tell us something they know about second grade?
Laura:	I know you're my teacher.
Evan:	I'm happy Laura is in my class.
Jacqui:	I think we get homework.
Mrs. Danoff:	Oh, that might be the second question: "What would you like to know about second grade?"
Laura:	Do we get homework?
Mrs. Danoff:	Yes!

Jacqui:	Do we have gym?
Thomas:	When is lunch?
Evan:	Will you answer our questions?
Mrs. Danoff:	Yes, of course I'll always try to answer your questions. But let's continue—then we can find out more. I want to know what you would like to learn this year in second grade.
Laura:	I want to learn how to read chapter books.
Evan:	Me, too, and really hard ones!
Zander:	I'd like to write better.
Mrs. Danoff:	I'm glad you said that, Zander, because we can start writing right now! In second grade, you'll each have your own personal writing journal in which you can write about many things all year. The letters I write to you this year are my journal. I am writing it to you. You can begin writing in your journals by answering my questions and asking questions about second grade. Then we can share our writing.
Jacqui:	Can we do that now?
Evan:	Then you'll answer our questions?
Mrs. Danoff:	Yes, here's a brand new journal for each one of you. When we're finished writing, I'll be able to answer your questions about second grade. So ask what you want. This is your chance!
Thomas:	Cool!

In second grade, most sentences change from day to day. The letter can be written as a flow of your thoughts about second grade, how you feel, what your class is doing, how the class reacted to something, questions, plans, ideas, and so forth. That's why it can really feel like a journal you're writing to your class, and yet be a model for all kinds of writing.

Extension Activity

Hand out writing journals. Instruct children to look at the letter, copy each question, and answer each question one at a time. Encourage children to write at least two ideas for each question. Then, allow children to share their answers. Pictured are some results. For more about journal writing, see Chapter 5 (page 61).

This journal entry was written in response to the letter on page 25. ▷

9/7

What I know about second grade. I know who my techer is. I know my class. I know were my classroom is. And I know we have homework. And I know, I have a great techer.

What I'd like to know about second grade. I'd like to know more math. I'd like to know to read more. I'd like to know if we cellibat birthdays.

What I'd like to learn about second grade

I'd like to learn when we have gim, computer, music and art.

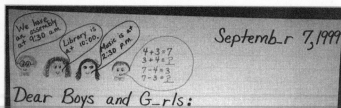

September_r 7, 1999

Dear Boys and G_rls:

This is our first day together. I am so excited!

I had a good summ__ but i could not wait for sch__l to start so that i could meet all of you. Today we will me_t each oth_r. You will get to know me bett_r, too, when you int_rview me this aft_rno_n. Hooray!

Tod_y we will share ideas about second grade. Do you expect it to be fun? Do you feel happy, scared, exc_t_d, or nervous?

Love,
Miss Duquette

Sept. 7, 1999

Good morning children,

Welcome to the (first) day of se*cond* grade! I am very excited about sharing this school year with you. Right now I feel happy and anxious to start discovering and learning many things. I cannot wait to begin!

How do you feel right now? Why? What are you looking forward to?

Have a great first day!

Love
Mrs. Diotte

THOUGHT FOR TODAY

More First-Day Letters

Pictured are first-day second-grade letters written by other teachers. Even though these teachers did not consult each other and some are even in different schools, you can see the similarities in language and ideas.

September 7, 1999

Dear Boys and Girls,

Good Morning! Welcome back to school. My name is Mrs. Carrozza and I am very excited to be your teacher this year! I can't wait to learn more about each one of you. Today I will show you around the classroom and the school so we all know where everything is! Miss Ducharme and I have lots of wonderful activities planned for all of you today. We have a lot to do so LET'S GET BUSY !! Have a terrific Tuesday!

Love,
Mrs. Carrozza

These first-day letters welcome students back to school and get them excited about learning.

Once you've introduced the Daily Letter, you're on your way to making it an integral part of your daily teaching. The chapters that follow focus on specific areas of learning and show you how a Daily Letter can pull everything together in your classroom.

How Daily Letters Change from September to June

O nce you've started writing Daily Letters to your class, it's important to consider how they will evolve during the year. In my nine years of writing Daily Letters to kindergarten, first-, and second-grade students, I've learned that pacing—of the writing and the content—is the key to success, and I remind myself every September to take it slow.

Children enter classrooms each year with clean slates, not knowing what to expect of their new teachers. Overwhelming them with a difficult letter that first day, week, or even month, can cause their interest and motivation to wane. While many children like a challenge, many do not, and I prefer to build their comfort level before asking them to take too many risks. Once they are comfortable, however, I do like to challenge students and stretch their thinking. To demonstrate what this looks like over the course of the year, I've chosen a range of letters below to show how the letter-writing process changes throughout the year.

Kindergarten Letters

Let's begin by looking at three letters written by Mrs. Lieberman to her kindergarten class. In her letter dated September 7, 1999, she has written only four sentences. She has placed stickers of a boy and girl above the words "Boys and Girls."

She has also drawn a clock for the time. This is a rebus technique to draw the children's attention to a familiar object. The sentences have very simple sentence structure.

Now compare this to her letter dated December 3, 1999 on page 31.

In just 56 days of school, she is comfortable writing seven sentences to her kindergartners. The class attention span has increased. They can probably identify which word says *girls* and which word says *boys*. The "Good morning!" with the rebus sun is still there, providing the security of knowing what to expect for those children who need it. She omits some words to be filled in by the class. If this were a color photo you would see that Mrs. Lieberman has maintained color switching for each sentence. She is dotting the numerals to count the days of school. She is repeating the sentence, "We have been in school for…"

September 7, 1999
Dear Boys and Girls,
Good morning!
Today is Terrific Tuesday.
It is a cloudy day. We have been in school for 1 day.
We have gym at 1:00.
Welcome to kindergarten!
Love,
Mrs. Lieberman

This first-day letter is perfect for kindergartners.

Compare this further to Mrs. Lieberman's letter dated January 24, 2000. Just about six weeks later she can omit the first letter of the word "Good," as well as the first letters of other words. She has also omitted the punctuation while still changing colors for sentences to indicate where the punctuation belongs.

You need to be the judge of the kinds of reading and writing skills your class is ready for and when to introduce them.

December 3, 1999

Dear Girls and Boys,
Good morning!
Today is Thoughtful Thursday. It is a ____ day. We have been in school for 36 thoughtful days.
____ is our thoughtful helper. ____ is our thoughtful caboose.
We will have a storyteller today. We also have library at 10:35.
Love,
Mrs. Lieberman

This letter reflects students' increased attention span.

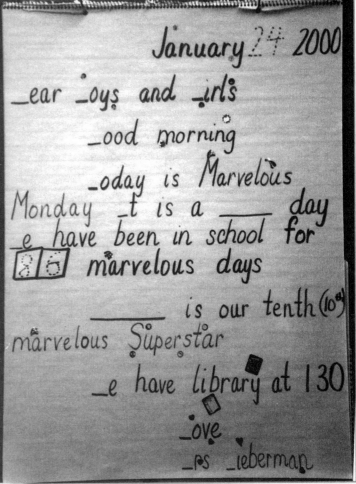

January 24 2000

_ear _oys and _irls
_ood morning
_oday is Marvelous Monday _t is a ____ day _e have been in school for 86 marvelous days
____ is our tenth (10th) marvelous Superstar
_e have library at 130
_ove
_rs _ieberman

Halfway through the year, these kindergartners are ready to fill in initial consonant sounds.

First-Grade Letters

Now look at some of the letters I wrote to my first graders. Though the spaces are filled in for the letter from November 16, 1993, you can tell by the line under certain letters which ones I had omitted.

I omitted the *G* in *Good*, the ending digraph *th*, the beginning digraph *sp*, the *es* and *day* in *yesterday*, the *to* in *today*, the *ed* in *enjoyed*, the *ue* in *blue*, the *y* in *sky*, the *un* in *Sunday*, and, again the digraph *th*, but this time as a beginning sound in *think*. These are all beginning sounds, chunks of familiar words, or blends that children work on during the first three months of first grade. The letter helped students review these concepts and let me informally assess their knowledge.

The letter dated February 18, 199_ demonstrates the progress first graders have made with language by the middle of the year.

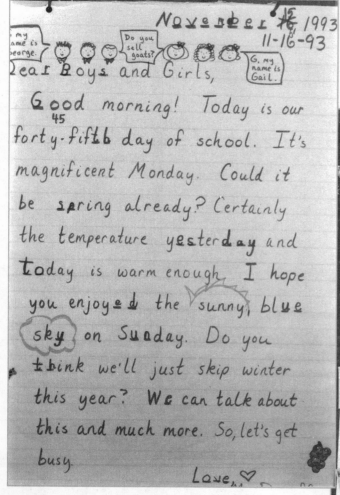

These first-grade letters illustrate the progress students made over three months.

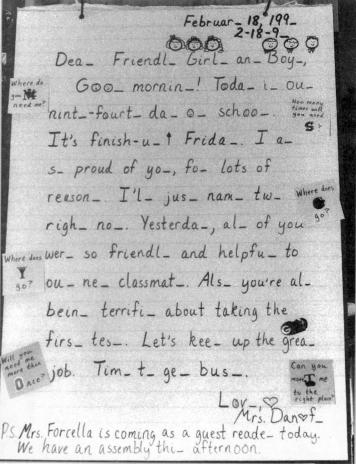

I was able to leave out many of the letters that represented the ending sounds of words. Of course there were some hints for letters on the sticky notes on the side. For instance, the one in the lower left-hand corner asks, "Will you need me more than once?" about the letter *o*. This letter shows an increase in attention span too. It takes much longer to fill in so many spaces.

The letter dated, May 2, 1994 amazes even me. There are so many spaces missing! Yet the children have absolutely no problem reading and thinking about what the words must be. They are ready for and truly enjoy the challenge the letter provides. They are comfortable taking risks in front of their classmates. They have a broader knowledge of vowel sounds and blends. They even recognize some spelling patterns.

By spring, students eagerly approach a challenging letter.

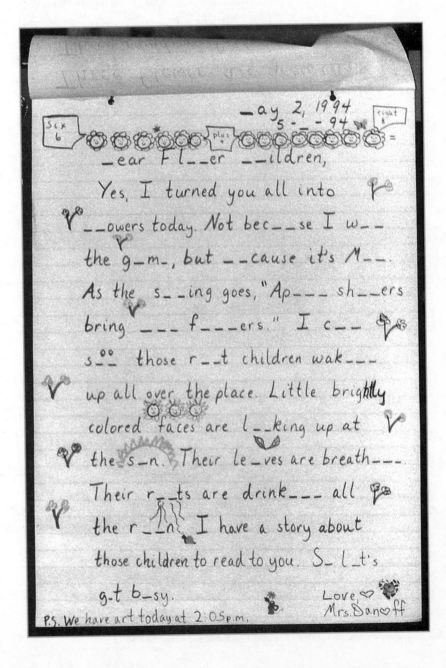

Second-Grade Letters

One last set of letters is worth a look. As I look at these letters now, I can see that the letters at the end of first grade look very similar to the letters at the beginning of second grade. However, that first-grade letter from May would not be what you would write to second graders at the very beginning of the year. Again, you need to entice them with simple text, gain their confidence, review their knowledge, and guide them into knowing what they know.

I've actually made the mistake during the first couple of weeks of school of writing a letter similar in terms of missing letters to the May letter on page 33. Not only did it make the second graders very uncomfortable, but some of them actually said they couldn't read it at all. They also did not have the patience, fresh from summer vacation, to sit through the process of filling in the letters.

The letter dated September 15, 1997, does not have as many missing spaces as the May first-grade letter above. Familiar blends such as *ee* and *oo* are omitted. Spelling patterns like *ow*, long vowel sounds like the *a* in *state*, digraphs like *st* in *best*, and common endings like *ing* and *ed* are fairly typical of what could be omitted at this time of year. That year I had about eight children who were extremely accurate spellers. They needed some challenging words, like *stadium* and *beautiful*, right away.

The letter dated December 8, 199_ , on page 35, illustrates the progress both in reading and writing that the children made since September. Now this looks more like the May letter on page 33 in terms of spaces omitted. The missing vowels, diphthongs, spelling patterns, and digraphs stress spelling words and the integration of vocabulary with our social studies food theme.

The children work with these theme words in large- and small-group reading, writing, and spelling activities. Words such as *they, say, which, little,* and *would* were on our high-frequency spelling words list. Changing the root word to add the ending *ing* as in *rise:rising* and *get:getting* was introduced as well. All of this can be easily worked into a letter by December.

Written early in the year, this second-grade letter provided plenty of support for students.

___ber 8, 199_

Dear Boys and Girls,

Well th_y s_y the temperature will be more s__sonal today. Rea__y that means the ther____eter won't r_s_ above 45°. Some r__n is mov____ in t___.

I gu___ we're all get___ ready to be s__d__ch chefs t_morrow. Do you think that p__n_t b_tt__, ch__se and l_tt___ on rye br___ would be good? Or w__l_ you like mayonnaise, t__k__ and cr__m ch__se on pita _rea_? Maybe you'd like t_m_t_, p_n__butter and b___er on wh_t_ br__d. Wh____ one would you tr_?

Love,
Mrs. Danoff

This spring letter incorporates social studies content and challenges students' editing skills.

april 14, 1999

dear Girls and boys, I really could'nt bee leave it yesterday. when i want running I saw so many of the animals were studying First of all, they're were more dear out then I've scene in a long time. Usually you donn't sea that many on a sonny day. Than I saw a read taled hawk circling above me in the bright blew sky. Finally on my whey home a wild turkey flu across the rode. It was a big won two. Its just so incredible too sea the ainimals around hear!

Love,
Mrs. Danoff

Finally, look at the Wacky Wednesday letter dated April 14, 1999.

As you read and look at this letter, you can imagine the amount of trust and risk-taking skill the children have acquired by now, not to mention the knowledge of spelling and language mechanics. It pulls in the content of our social studies unit, Community Animals, and is filled with examples of descriptive writing. The children have become such good and confident spellers that they actually laugh out loud as they read this letter. They're excited to demonstrate their knowledge. They are now capable and ready for this kind of letter.

As you read the following chapters and as you introduce early letters, refer to this section every now and then to help keep a sense of perspective.

4

Making Every Day Special

The Daily Letter can help you make every day special. I like naming each day of the week: Marvelous Monday gets our week off to a great start, and Finish-Up Friday gives us all a sense of closure. The days in between continue the mix of word play and learning, from Tangled Tuesday to Wacky Wednesday to Thinking Thursday. Using alliterative names is fun, and naming each day builds excitement and anticipation. Even though each day has a predictable name, you can integrate any skills you want at any time. You also have the flexibility of writing an extra-special letter to recognize extra-special days—Daily Letters are a great way to introduce special events, launch theme units, or recap a field trip or outing.

In this chapter I share some of the ways I've discovered to make every day sparkle with a Daily Letter.

Marvelous Monday

Children return to school every Monday filled with wonderful weekend adventures. A marvelous thing to do on a Marvelous Monday is to give children an opportunity to tell the class about their weekends. The letter dated January 24, 2000, is an example of a second-grade letter meant to spark conversations about weekend activities; the next chapter, about writing, details how a Monday letter helps children write weekend notes.

J_____ 24, 2000

Dear Boys and Girls,

Happy M_____y! My w__k__d was sort of busy. I actually had to take a test early S_t__day morning. I'm studying about p__ple who speak two languages. As part of my study, I needed to be tested in English. I had to listen to taped conversat____ and answer quest____ about what the p__p_e were saying. I had to be a very good listener!

I was also thinking about our poetry writing over the weekend. For our ur__n poem we can learn how to wr_t_ a cinquain. If you think ab__t languages you may have h___rd, think about counting. Th_n you might guess how many l_n_s are in a cinquain.

Love, Mrs. Danoff

This Marvelous Monday letter sparked discussion about the weekend and then led into our poetry unit.

Dear Boys ___ Girls,   _anuary __, 20__

Good morn___! Today __ marvelous _onday. We have been in school for ___ days. There are _tens and _ones. We have reading groups today and Ms. Brady will be coming in to work with us. We will also be learning about more animals and how they survive in winter. Do you remember what hibernate and migrate mean?

Love, Mrs. Carrozza

Mrs. Carozza's combined first- and second-grade class for children with special needs enjoyed this Marvelous Monday letter.

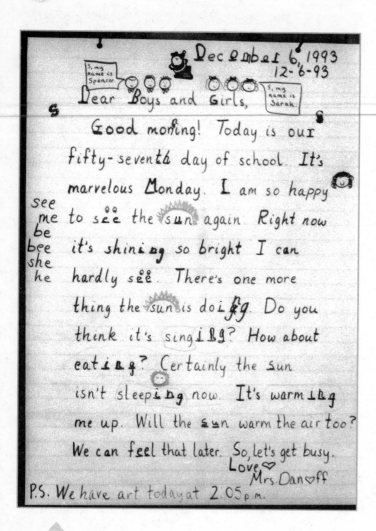

A Happy Day letter welcomes children back from a weekend in December.

A Fresh Start

The letter dated December 6, 1993, illustrates a typical Marvelous Monday letter from first grade. Although the weather had been dreary and we were feeling dull, the letter helped us jumpstart our week by plunging us into a lively discussion of science and word endings.

Skills

* *ing* ending
* words rhyming with *see*. The children were made aware of the different spelling pattern.
* building curiosity about a science topic (temperature)

Extension Activities

* Make a list of words to which you can add *ing* by dropping an *e* or without adding a consonant. There are other words in the letter, such as *think, will,* and *feel,* that can start the list.
* Make a list of rhyming words. Choose a word with a spelling pattern you want to introduce, review, or explore.

Refreshing Our Memories

The letter dated February 7, 1994, on page 39, is a Marvelous Monday letter that gets children ready to begin another week. It reminds children about the projects they need to complete, and the activities—like guessing candy hearts—that are available in the classroom. As we read each sentence together, we discuss who has to complete what.

Skills

* long and short vowel sounds, *cvce* pattern (consonant, vowel, consonant, silent *e*) as in *take* and *time*
* review of classroom projects and activities that are available and need to be completed

Lesson Excerpt

Mrs. Danoff: Has everyone had a chance to read the letter to themselves? Thumbs up if you have.

Class indicates by thumbs up that they are ready.

Mrs. Danoff: Well, do you agree? Is it a Marvelous Monday? I just love a sunny day. What's the number of today's school day from the letter?

Angela: [raising her hand] 86th.

Mrs. Danoff: Great! Is that a number we can get to if we count by fives, tens, or twos?

Class: Twos!

Mrs. Danoff: Let's do that then.

Together: 2, 4, 6, 8, 10, 12, etc.

Mrs. Danoff: Wow! You're becoming very good counters. Let's continue and read the letter together.

Class reads the letter chorally.

Payton: How come you wrote *2day is our eighty-sixth day of school* instead of the whole word? I thought you said we can't mix numbers with letters to write a word.

Mrs. Danoff: Yes that's true, but I wanted to remember to count by twos today and we did. So how would you really spell *today*?

Payton: T-o-d-a-y.

Mrs. Danoff: Good for you. Come up and write that on the letter for us above *2day*.

Payton comes up and writes the word correctly.

Mrs. Danoff: George, you're the special helper today. Come up and help us spell *dear*.

As George writes the whole class spells dear together. Children continue coming up to fill in letters as the class spells together.

Mrs. Danoff: What two letters are missing at the end of the word *such*?

Alice: *ch*

Mrs. Danoff: That's right, because *c* and *h* got married and now they're *ch*. Raise your hand if you see another word in the letter that has the same ending.

Tim: [raises hand and is called on] *much*

Mrs. Danoff: Good for you! Come on up and fill in the *ch* for us.

As Tim comes up to complete the word the class spells the whole word together.

Mrs. Danoff: Raise your hand if you can think of another word that ends with *ch*.

John: *Touch*

Enid: *Bunch*

Alvin: *Crunch*

Several children have turns, and I continue filling in more words.

_ebru___ 7, 1994
-7-94

D__r Love__ L_dies and Gentlem_n,
Good morning! 2day is our eighty-
sixth day of s_____. It's su__
a s_nny marvelous M_____. It's
the beginn___ of another w__k of
school. There's only ___ more week
until ♥_ _entin_'s Day. I hop_
all of you have the tim_ to
mak_ a ♡alentine P_L this week.
I c_n s°° a few of you have.
Also, don't forget to tak_ a guess
about the candy hearts and fill a
candy Valentine. So mu__ to do. So l_t's
g_t busy.   Love,♥ Mrs. Dan♥ff

P.s. We have art today at 2:05 p.m.

I reminded students about our plans for the week in this Monday letter.

Mrs. Danoff:	[After filling in the letters for *Valentine*, *hope*, and *time*] Raise your hand if you know the answer to this question: What do the words *Valentine*, *hope*, and *time* have in common?
Chris:	[raises hand and is called on] They all end with *e*.
Mrs. Danoff:	That's right! So that usually makes the other vowel in the word or syllable say its name. You may remember we talked about this before. It's a good thing to try when reading a new word too. Raise your hand if you can find another word in the letter that ends with *e*.
Peter:	Well, I think *make* does.
Mrs. Danoff:	Good for you, Peter. Come up and fill that letter in. [Peter fills in the letter as the whole class spells the whole word.] Now, raise your hand if you can find the word that rhymes with *make* and is also missing an *e*.
Kelly:	I know it's *take*. Can I fill in the letter even though we're not up to it yet?
Mrs. Danoff:	You're a good word detective, Kelly. Sure, come up and fill in the letter.

The children and I continue this way, filling in the missing letters.

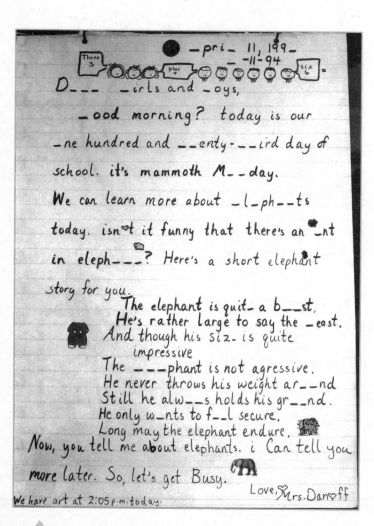

A Mammoth Monday letter focused on capitalization.

Follow-up

I take a count of those who have not completed their Valentine Pals or visited the Valentine Center to make a guess, and then remind those children to make time to get there. We compile a list of words that rhyme with *make*. Then we point out words that have the *cvce* pattern.

More Ways to Make Monday Marvelous

While a Marvelous Monday letter is always an upbeat way to start the week, there are more fun twists you can try. During one of the years I taught first grade, I instituted Mammoth Monday because I wanted to focus on capitalization. I would gradually introduce skills like capitalizing the first letter of a sentence or capitalizing names—making these letters mammoth. Then, every Monday, the Daily Letter would reinforce the capitalization skills we'd worked on. As in the letter at left, I left the first letter of several words blank so we could talk about which ones should be capitalized and why. I also began the first word of a sentence with a lowercase letter to see if students would notice.

Tangled Tuesday

Tuesday can be terrific with a Daily Letter. I like to make it even more interesting by "tangling" words—hence the name Tangled Tuesday. I simply scramble words in the letter, and students use context clues and phonics skills to unscramble them. This is also a handy tool to use when you have to be away—simply scramble a list of spelling or vocabulary words for students to untangle on their own or with a partner. Students of all ages love this challenge, but be sure to make words for younger readers less tangled than those for older readers. The letter below features spelling words for a second-grade class.

Tangling Words

The letter at right helped students review spelling words while I attended a meeting. When I returned, we read the letter together.

Skills

* spelling
* phonics

Sample Lesson

Mrs. Danoff: Peri, you're the special helper today, will you please read the first sentence.

Peri: [Reads] Oh, that's a tangled word already. But I know it because it's one of our spelling words. But it looks so funny that way!

Maria: I love Tangled Tuesday.

Enid: Yeah! This is so fun!

Josh: I think I'm getting better at it.

Noah: I don't know, I just can't figure some of those words out. Hey! *Raccoon* needs another *c*.

Mrs. Danoff: Okay, let's just take it one line at a time. I'm glad you all like this so much; you're becoming very good at it. I have to tell you, sometimes it's hard to tangle all the words and get all the letters in. I guess you can see what happens when you write in a hurry—you can leave letters out. Good for you for seeing that, Noah. That earns you reading the next sentence.

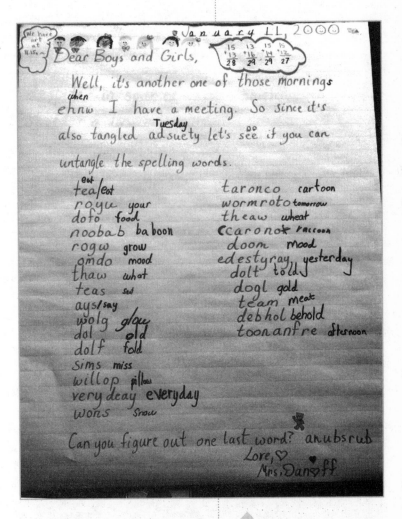

Tangling spelling words is a fun review activity.

Noah:	[Reads] Oh, I know that's *Tuesday* even though it doesn't have a capital letter.
Mrs. Danoff:	Okay, now let's pretend these are all new words that we've never seen before and we have to sound them out.
Stephanie:	Well then we'd have to go to the dictionary to see what they mean, because I don't know what *noobab* means!
Mrs. Danoff:	You're right. Let's see which word sounds the funniest. Also, can you see a word that spells another word when it's tangled? [*teas* spells *seat*] Sometimes the same letters make a different word. My favorite one is h-e-a-r-t.
Rachel	That spells *heart*.
Mrs. Danoff:	Yes, I'll write it on the board and later you can tell me what other word these letters spell. [*earth*]

The class continues pronouncing all the tangled words. It's great practice for sounding out words, especially for second graders who rely on this skill less and less as they become more and more fluent. However, they still need to be able to do it to decode new vocabulary words.

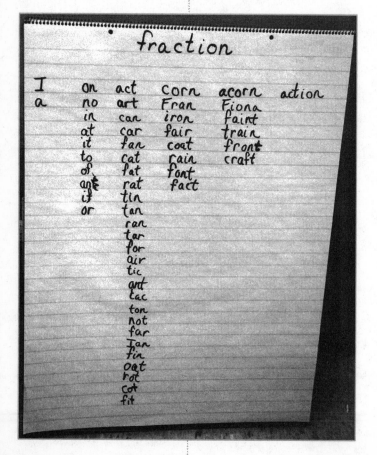

Follow-up

A follow-up activity that I did with this letter (but that you could do on any day) was to see how many small words the class could make out of the last tangled word: *anubsrub*. This word stumped my kids, so we started by making 2-, 3-, 4-, and 5-letter words from the scrambled letters, and eventually they came up with *suburban* (which was one of their vocabulary words).

◀ *Students make words from the letters of* fraction. *You can extend this activity even further by brainstorming rhyming words to the words you create.*

A Terrific Tangled Tuesday

The photos from February 8, 2000, show how you can combine the terrific idea with the tangled idea—and pack in lots of learning. We reviewed our spelling words by untangling them, revisited contractions, and worked on vowel sounds and word endings. While we were filling in the letter, Anne noted that the third sentence should say *you worked*. She thought the ending sound was a *t*, but there were two spaces for it.

Skills

✷ ending sounds   ✷ spelling patterns

Sample Lesson

Anne: So *worked* must be one of those words that ends in *ed* even though it sounds like /t/. There are lots of them!

Mrs. Danoff: Yes, there are. In fact, most words that make that sound when they mean something happened in the past do end in *ed*. Can you think of some words that do change to a *t*?

Cyrus: *Worked?*

Mrs. Danoff: Well it sounds like a *t* for sure, but keep thinking.

Alison: How about *slept* then?

Mrs. Danoff: Good! I'll write that one down. Who can think of another one?

Cyrus: How about *wept?*

Mrs. Danoff: Yes, Cyrus that does change. Do you know what the word is that it changes from?

Cyrus: *Weeped?*

Mrs. Danoff: Well it's *weep* that changes to *wept* if it happened say, yesterday.

We continued to brainstorm verbs that change to *t* or *pt* when put in the past. The margin of the letter is a perfect place to add such a list. After we listed the words, the children circled or underlined words with the same spelling pattern change.

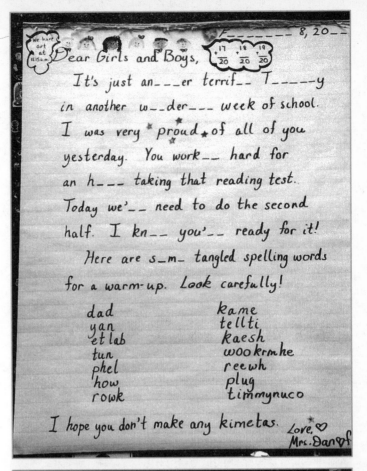

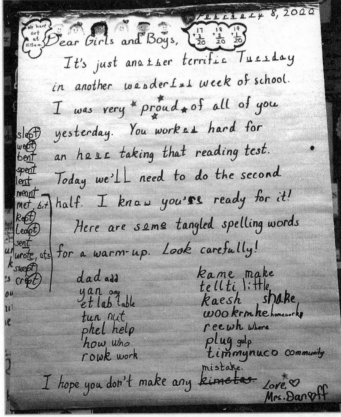

The before and after photos of this letter show how interactive the Daily Letter can be. Kids came up to unscramble spelling words, and the class brainstormed words ending in pt.

Wacky Wednesday

I have found that's it's best to have a certain day set aside to practice editing skills and establish expectations for written work. I've named that day Wacky Wednesday because of all the funny mistakes that are the hallmark of such letters.

Mrs. Liebermann's kindergartners were treated to a multi-colored Wacky Wednesday letter that began with a closing.

Wackiness Works

The first Wacky Wednesday letter is always a surprise for children. That a teacher could make a mistake or write something so silly startles students. This is the first wacky letter I wrote to my second graders last year. Once they recovered from their surprise, however, they learned valuable editing techniques.

Skills

✳ editing

✳ spelling

✳ homonyms

My second graders learn editing skills with Wacky Wednesday letters.

Sample Lesson

Jesse: [Before the teacher can even say anything] Oh, look at the girls and boys—they're upside down!

Marta: I see a mistake in the letter today. You wrote the wrong *see*.

Mrs. Danoff: That's because today is… Well, you tell me. What does the letter say about that?

Alison: Oh, I see it says that it's Wacky Wednesday. But what does that mean?

Mrs. Danoff: What does anybody think that might mean in this letter?

Zander: I guess it means there are some funny things because the girls and boys really do look funny upside down!

Noah: Well, I see mistakes so maybe there are mistakes in the letter today.

Lizzie: I read the letter and it says you made spelling and punctuation mistakes that we need to correct.

Mrs. Danoff: That's right. You're all right! The Wacky Wednesday letter has spelling and punctuation mistakes. Just like I will help you edit your writing for mistakes, you will help me edit my letter for mistakes. And just like I will edit your work as neatly as possible so you can use your rough draft for a final copy, we need to edit this letter as neatly as possible. Now, I want to tell you that when I make a spelling mistake in the Wacky Wednesday letter, it's because…You know what, let's read the letter. I wonder if you can see what kind of spelling mistakes I've made today. Kathy, will you read the first sentence please?

Kathy reads the first sentence, and children take turns reading sentences in the letter until…

Danielle: [Reads] *you help me edit just like I'll bee helping you.* Shouldn't the *y* in *you* be upper case because that's beginning a sentence?

Mrs. Danoff: Yes, Danielle you're right. Would you like to come up here and fix it? What's the neatest way you could change that *y* to upper case?

Danielle: I could cross it out, then write above it.

Mrs. Danoff: Okay, let's try that. What color marker do you think would show up best. [The letter is written in green.]

Danielle: I think black would work. [Danielle comes up and makes the change.]

Stephanie: Is that the right *be*? Isn't that the buzzy bee that stings you?

Mrs. Danoff: You're right Stephanie. What is the correct spelling?

Stephanie: b-e. Can I come up and correct that?

Mrs. Danoff: Sure. What is the neatest way to make that a correction?

Stephanie: I could just cross out one *e*.

Mrs. Danoff: Great! Go ahead.

Stephanie makes the correction.

Mrs. Danoff: Evan, will you read the next sentence please?

Evan: [Reads, but quickly says] Oh, I see it's the wrong *see*. You gave us a hint by drawing the waves, and the fish sticker too. Can I come up and fix it?

Mrs. Danoff: Good for you Evan. So which *see* did I write?

Evan: You wrote the one that's like the ocean.

Mrs. Danoff: And which *see* should be written in this sentence?

Evan: The *see* with your eyes. Can I fix it now?

Mrs. Danoff: Come on up, but remember to be neat.

Evan makes the correction. Children read the next two sentences. Then…

Chris: Oh, I see, the eyeball in the next sentence is a hint.

Mrs. Danoff: Why do you say that?

Chris: Because it should be the *I* like me, not that *eye*.

Mrs. Danoff: What *eye* is that?

Chris: That's the eyeball kind of eye. Can I fix it?

Mrs. Danoff: You're absolutely right, Chris, good for you. Yes, come on up and fix that, but remember to be neat.

Once the letter is complete…

Mrs. Danoff: Now, girls and boys, did I really spell any words wrong?

Zander: Well, you did, but you didn't.

Stephanie: They were the wrong words but the spelling was right.

Noah: You spelled them wrong because they were the wrong words.

Anne: They sounded like the right word, but they weren't spelled like the right word.

Mrs. Danoff: Actually, you're all correct. Has anyone ever heard of a homonym?

There's a mixed reaction from the class.

Mrs. Danoff: Homonyms are different words that are pronounced and can even be spelled the same.

Anne: You mean they're different words but they're the same words? Then what's the difference?

Mrs. Danoff: The difference is that they mean something different. For instance, look at the word *see*. Who can tell me another one like this from the letter?

Lizzie: Is *I* one?

Mrs. Danoff: Yes, good for you! I'm going to make our very first reference chart. That's a chart that we can use again and again. This one is going to be about homonyms. [Takes a flip chart and writes *homonym* and the definition.] Okay, with which words can we start our list?

Lizzie: *I* and *eye*

Mrs. Danoff: Great. Any others?

Anne: Does it have to be in the letter? Because I can think of *witch* like the witch that flies, and *which* when you mean which one.

Mrs. Danoff: You've caught on. I'll write down *witch* and *which* but then let's go back to the words in the letter.

The class continues this way.

Mrs. Danoff: Okay, that's great for today. We can add to this list as we come across other homonyms.

Extension Activities

Read aloud the book, *Wacky Wednesday* by Theodore Lesieg (Random House, 1974)

Write a homonym chart as described above. Add to it as the year goes on, and encourage children to keep their own list in the back of their writing journals.

Wise Wackiness

Children and teachers alike enjoy finding and correcting the funny mistakes in wacky letters. I often remind myself, however, to always reinforce spelling patterns and punctuation rules and teach editing skills. I now prefer to use homonyms as the "misspellings." (See letter at right.) This way children really do not see any misspelled words, which can be very confusing for them.

In addition to teaching and reviewing spelling patterns, homonyms, and editing skills, you can integrate social studies and science concepts by writing about a content-area topic you're teaching. See the letters dated January 19 and April 14 as examples.

Homonyms make great editing challenges and review spelling words.

▶

These letters helped us practice editing skills while reading about social studies and science topics.

▼

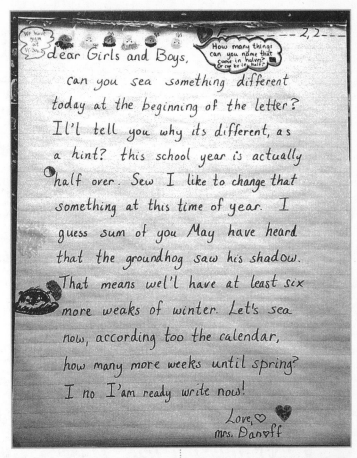

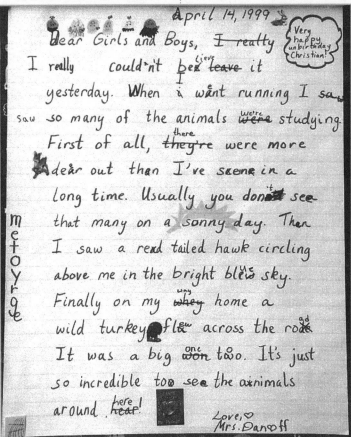

Thinking Thursday

How can you top Wacky Wednesday? Why, with Thinking Thursday, of course! I like to focus my Thinking Thursday letters on math. This emphasis allows me to introduce, practice, or review a math concept, and I can also bring in a theme we're working on. I incorporate math concepts into letters on other days, too, but the math focus makes Thursdays special.

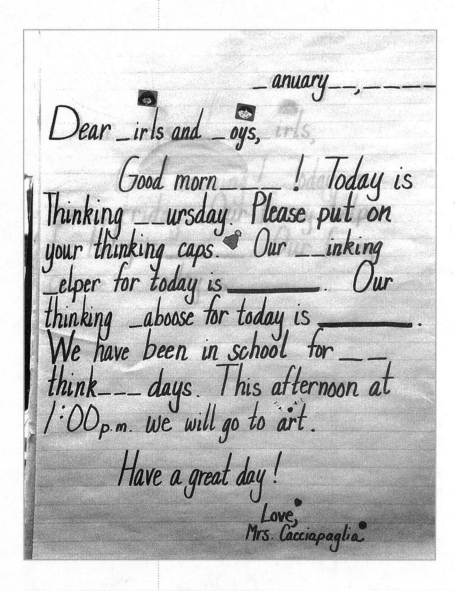

_anuary___,_____

Dear _irls and _oys,

    Good morn_____ ! Today is Thinking __ursday. Please put on your thinking caps. Our __inking _elper for today is _____. Our thinking _aboose for today is _____. We have been in school for __ think___ days. This afternoon at 1:00 p.m. we will go to art.

    Have a great day !

Love,
Mrs. Cacciapaglia

Pictured here is Mrs. Cacciapaglia's idea of Thinking Thursday for her kindergarten class. Her focus here is the th digraph.

Adding Apples

Here are some skills and extension activities to get Thinking Thursday off to a good start. The letter and lesson are from a first-grade class. The day before, we had gone apple-picking to study farms and use math skills in the real world.

Skills

* sorting
* equalizing
* patterning

Sample Lesson

Mrs. Danoff: Let's count the boys and girls today. Is everybody here? Hannah, will you begin by being number one please?

Hannah: One.

The children continue as I point to them until everyone is counted.

Mrs. Danoff: Well, we only got up to the number 16. We have eighteen children in our class. So let's see, how many children are absent today? Let's look at the eighteen children I drew on the letter and count up to 16. [The class counts together.] How many children are left?

Ben: Two.

Mrs. Danoff: Okay. Now let's count on and make sure we can get to eighteen. [The class completes the counting.] Now let's read the rest of the letter together because there is more counting to do today!

The class read the letter chorally and filled in the spaces. Then I returned to the math questions posed and the bubble question. After the class considered the pattern in the letter, we went right into a full group math lesson with the apples we had picked the day before.

Extension Activity

Using real or paper apples—or any other manipulative math material—sort by color and pattern, and count to see how to equalize the amount of materials among children.

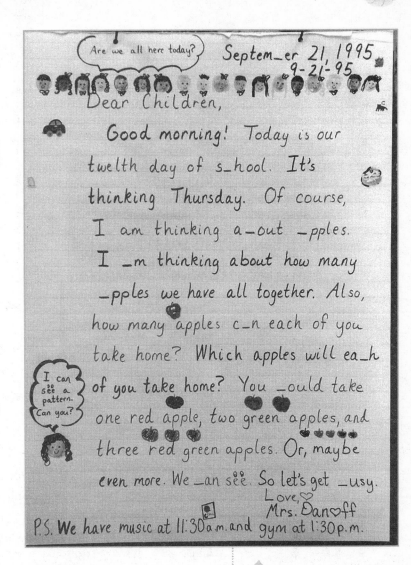

Are we all here today? September 21, 1995
9-21-95

Dear Children,

Good morning! Today is our twelfth day of s_hool. It's thinking Thursday. Of course, I am thinking a_out _pples. I _m thinking about how many _pples we have all together. Also, how many apples c_n each of you take home? Which apples will ea_h of you take home? You _ould take one red apple, two green apples, and three red green apples. Or, maybe even more. We _an see. So let's get _usy.

I can see a pattern. Can you?

Love,
Mrs. Danoff

P.S. We have music at 11:30 a.m. and gym at 1:30 p.m.

My first graders enjoyed finding the pattern I made by alternating the colors of the apples.

Solving Stories

This next letter sets up a story problem involving measurement and addition.

Skills

* measurement
* addition
* counting on

Sample Lesson

The class reads the letter up to the question about how much snow has fallen altogether.

Mrs. Danoff: Let's look at the yardstick to help us figure this out. You've seen it before. We can use it just like a ruler to measure inches. How many inches does the yardstick go up to? [See the yardstick on the left in the picture.]

Peter: Is it 36"? I see 36 up at the top.

Mrs. Danoff: That's right. Now look at this ruler. How many inches does it go up to?

Angie: It says 12 right there, so I guess it's twelve.

Mrs. Danoff: That's right! So would it be easier to measure something that's more than twelve inches with a ruler or a yardstick?

Carol: A yardstick, because it's bigger.

Mrs. Danoff: That's right. But for now, who would like to come up and show us where the number four is on this yardstick?

Sarah comes up and points to the number four.

Mrs. Danoff: Good, Sarah now keep your finger there. Who can count on to three more inches so we can see how many inches fell altogether?

Evan: Do I just go 1, 2, 3?

Mrs. Danoff: What do you think Evan should do, everyone? Where can he start his counting?

Sarah: I'm already at the four, so he can't start at the one to count on.

Mrs. Danoff: Good for you. Evan come up and start at the four then count on from there.

Evan: Should I just go up to the seven because I know that 3 + 4 = 7?

Mrs. Danoff: Yes, you're right and we will get to the seven, but count each inch so we can see how we get there.

Evan counts up to seven, and we continue reading the letter.

A recent snowfall provided an excellent opportunity to practice our measurement skills on this Thinking Thursday.

Thinking Thursday Extension Activities

FOR MEASUREMENT:

✳ Give more children turns to come up to the yardstick to show inches and counting on. Change the numbers or add on more numbers by saying, "What if two more inches falls tonight? Then how many inches would be on the ground?" Or, "Now all the snow has melted. We can start again. What if two inches falls tonight and four more inches fall the next night?"

✳ Give each child a ruler to look at inches and measure things in the room. Of course, more measurement activities would follow.

✳ Read aloud *Inch by Inch* by Leo Lionni (Mulberry Books, 1995).

This letter uses a thermometer to practice the same skills. You can see too that the heart stickers were used to help the children figure out the story problem.

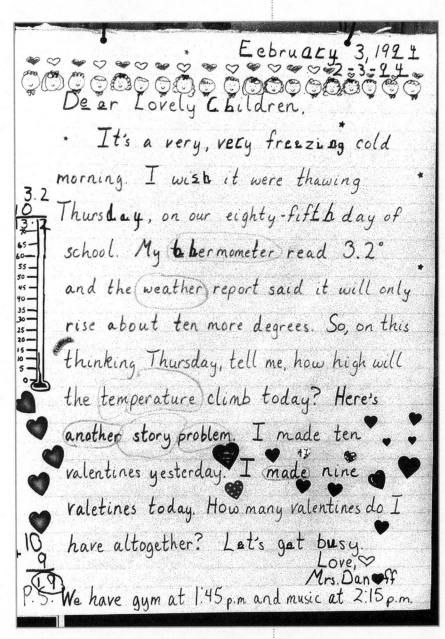

February 3, 1994
2-3-94

Dear Lovely Children,

It's a very, very freezing cold morning. I wish it were thawing Thursday, on our eighty-fifth day of school. My thermometer read 3.2° and the weather report said it will only rise about ten more degrees. So, on this thinking Thursday, tell me, how high will the temperature climb today? Here's another story problem. I made ten valentines yesterday. I made nine valentines today. How many valentines do I have altogether? Let's get busy.
Love,
Mrs. Danoff

P.S. We have gym at 1:45 p.m. and music at 2:15 p.m.

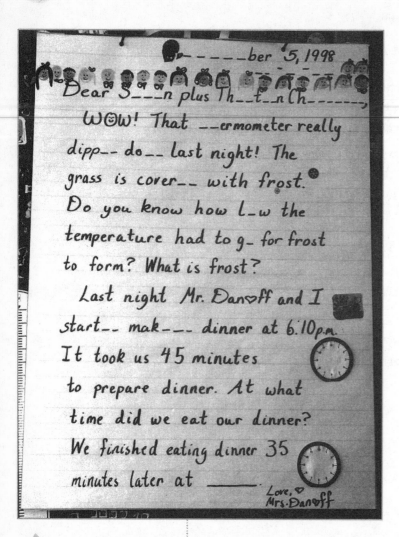

The children love coming up and drawing the hands on the clocks.

FOR TIME:

✳ Give children their own manipulative analog clocks (available from many school catalogs). Have them practice setting the times stated in the letter and other times throughout the day. Give the children clocks on which to draw the hands.

✳ Ask children to write down the their daily schedule and how long it takes them to do each thing.

✳ Read aloud *Nine O'Clock Lullaby* by Marilyn Singer (Harper Trophy, 1991), *Clocks and More Clocks* by Pat Hutchins (Macmillan, 1970), *8 o'clock* by Jill Creighton (Scholastic, 1995), or *All in a Day* by Mitsumasa Anno (Penguin, 1986).

FOR TEMPERATURE:

✳ Put water of varying temperatures in containers. Have the children work in groups with small thermometers to read the temperatures.

✳ Hang a thermometer outside your window. Make it part of your day to check the morning and afternoon temperature. Finish the day with a math problem computing the difference between the morning and afternoon temperature.

FOR STORY PROBLEMS:

✳ Give children manipulative math materials to perform the functions themselves.

✳ Ask children to write their own story problems every Thursday night for homework. Then, on Fridays, share these with the class at math time.

✳ Read aloud *My Little Sister Ate One Hare* by Bill Grossman (Crown Publishers, 1996), or *Bunches and Bunches of Bunnies* by Louise Mathews (Dodd Mead & Co., 1978).

Estimating Combinations

The letter dated December 3, 1998, has an interesting twist and a fun follow-up, especially if you decide to make sandwiches, as we did.

Skills

* variations
* combination
* estimating

Sample Lesson

Mrs. Danoff: I'm getting hungry just thinking about what I wrote in my letter today. Let's all read it quietly to ourselves. Thumbs up when you're finished.

Arieh: I'm hungry, too, just looking at all those foods!

Mrs. Danoff: [After most thumbs are up] Jeffrey will you please read the first sentence out loud for us?

Jeffrey: [Reads then says] Yeah! I thought about that yesterday. Like what do I want in my sandwich?

Mrs. Danoff: Yes, there are many possibilities [I said *possibilities* to be of some help with the next sentence]. Emily, please read the next sentence.

Emily: *I kind of got very faasss-kin*

Mrs. Danoff: Good for you, Emily. The *c* is soft in front of an *i*. Everybody, let's look at that word. [Uses a piece of sentence strip to cover up syllables and aid in decoding the word.] Emily is right. *fas* is pronounced *fas*, soft *c* then *in* [the class pronounces it correctly, as *cin*].

Emily: Oh, I know now. It's *fascinated*.

Mrs. Danoff: Yes, good for you!

Emily: [Continues reading] *poss- possi- possibly- oh possibilities.* What you said before!

Mrs. Danoff: Yes! Does everyone know what *possibilities* means?

Andres: I'm not sure what *fascinated* means.

Mrs. Danoff: That means I really couldn't stop thinking about something and I really liked that idea too. Do you want to get the dictionary, and we'll see what it says?

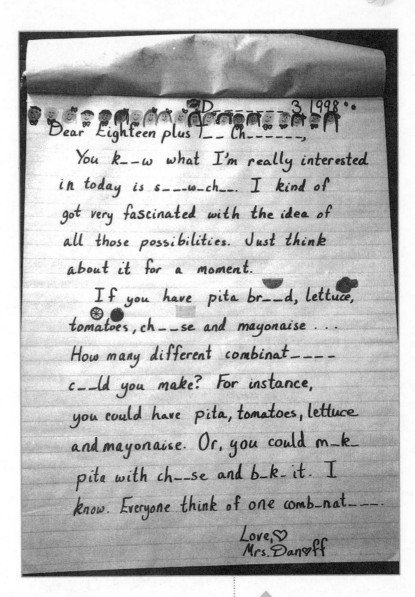

Making sandwiches provided the inspiration for this letter on estimation.

Andres gets a dictionary and the teacher assists in looking up the word and reading the definition to the class.

Mrs. Danoff: Okay, good, Andres. Now let's think about the word *possibilities*.

Jeffrey: That means different ways of doing things. You wrote that in the letter, too.

Mrs. Danoff: You're right, Jeffrey. I guess you've already thought about it.

The class continues reading the letter.

Extension Activities

✳ Invite children to estimate the number of sandwich possibilities from a certain number of ingredients. Then, record student-suggested combinations on chart paper. Finally, compare the estimated number with the actual number of combinations.

✳ Follow up by really making the sandwiches!

✳ Ask children to list their four or five favorite ingredients and then come up with as many combinations as they can, using that list.

✳ Read the books *1001 Silly Sandwiches* by Alan Benjamin (Simon & Schuster, 1995) or *Ketchup on Your Corn Flakes* by Nick Sharratt (Scholastic, 1994).

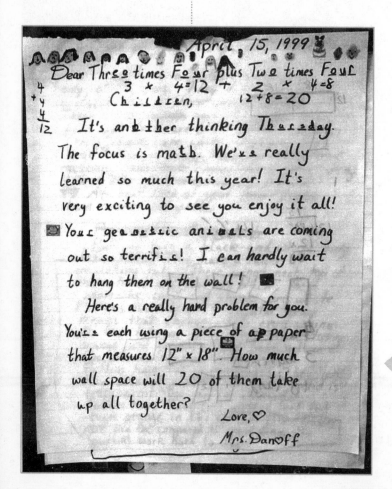

Computing Area

There was heated discussion as to how to solve the problem presented in the letter at left. I wanted students to figure out how big a bulletin board would have to be to hold everyone's geometric animal. My students concluded that we would have to add 18 twenty times if we wanted to go width wise and that we should allow enough space for that possibility. However, they quickly realized that not everybody had placed their illustration to hang width wise. So after allowing for the maximum, everybody decided to try out different arrangements using a piece of plain white paper.

◀ *Thinking Thursdays are a great time to pull together all the math skills students have learned and apply them to a fun problem, as I do in the second paragraph of this letter.*

Fantastic Friday

Friday can be "Finish-up" or "Fickle" or just plain "Fun." No matter what you call it, everyone is happy when it arrives. Friday is a good day to wrap up the whole week. In first grade, concentrating on the last letter of each word, the letter that "finishes up" the word, was great fun for the class and an excellent teaching tool for emergent readers. Not only does it help children practice sounding out words, it also reinforces spelling patterns.

Fickle Friday

You can also write Fickle Friday letters, which I have used to teach and review homonyms. Typically, I start these letters in the late spring of first grade, when students have enough word knowledge to identify homonym pairs. See the photo on the top of page 56 for a sample first grade letter.

In second grade I begin Fickle Friday letters in the late fall. Often the subject of these letters is our week in school; it helps children with their journal entries. (See Chapter 5 for more on journal writing.) When introducing a Fickle Friday letter, I tell children they need to read all the words, so each homonym pair is read aloud. Every week children get a kick out of hearing both words said, and then we talk about which word is the right one for the sentence. After reading, children come up and circle the correct word.

Skills

* spelling
* homonyms
* punctuation
* expression

Sample Lesson

Anne: It's always so funny when we read the Fickle Friday letter!

Mrs. Danoff: That's because it sounds like people are double talking. Has everyone had time to read the letter to themselves? I see a lot of thumbs up. Noah, read the first sentence for us today.

Noah: [Reading] *We've, Weave had a short but busy weak week.*

The class continues reading the letter in this way. Then:

Mrs. Lieberman is sure to get a laugh with her lift-the-flap joke written especially for her kindergartners.

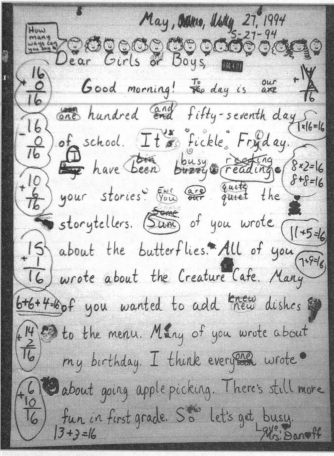

The two handwritten letters from Mrs. Danoff (with children's circled corrections, homophones, and math problems in the margins):

First letter:

May, ~~June, July~~ 27, 1994
5-27-94

Dear Girls or Boys,

Good morning! ~~To~~ To day is ~~our~~ are ~~one~~ hundred ~~and~~ and fifty-seventh day of school. It's "fickle" Fryday. I have ~~bin~~ been ~~buzzy~~ busy ~~reeding~~ reading your stories. ~~Ewe~~ You ~~are~~ our quiet the storytellers. ~~Sum~~ Some of you wrote about the butterflies. All of you wrote about the Creature Cafe. Many of you wanted to add ~~knew~~ new dishes to the menu. Many of you wrote about my birthday. I think every~~one~~ wrote about going apple picking. There's still more fun in first grade. So let's get busy.

Love, Mrs. Danoff

Margin math problems:
16 ⊙ 16 = 16
16 − 0 = 16
10 + 6 = 16
15 + 1 = 16
1×16 = 16
8×2 = 16
8+8 = 16
11 + 5 = 16
7 + 9 = 16
6+6+4 = 16
14 + 2 = 16
6 + 10 = 16
13 + 3 = 16

Second letter:

~~Dear~~ Deer Boys ~~end~~ and Girls, 21, ____

~~Weave~~ We've had a short but busy ~~weak~~ week. ~~Its~~ It's ~~knot~~ not over yet though. ~~Eye~~ I guess the snow ~~maid~~ made it very exciting ~~too~~ to. First of all, I have ~~two~~ to tell you that ~~your~~ you're Poetry Place performances were spectacular! You ~~are~~ our really working well together ~~too~~ to figure out how ~~to~~ two interpret the poems. Speaking of poems, you wrote fabulous poems about Bedford. You used the comparisons with ~~grate~~ great describing words ~~too~~ two. Reading The Big Orange Splot was ~~sew~~ so much fun. ~~You're~~ Your own dream houses are ~~sew~~ so terrific! I can hardly ~~weight~~ wait ~~too~~ to share them.

Love, Mrs. Danoff

Mrs. Danoff: Lizzie, you're the helper today, what color marker would you like to use to circle the correct words?

Lizzie: I'll take red.

Mrs. Danoff: That will show up with the blue nicely. Let's begin with the *Dear Deer*.

Lizzie circles Dear.

Mrs. Danoff: Lizzie, tell the class why you circled the *Dear* on top.

Lizzie: Because the one on the bottom— the *d-e-e-r*—is the deer that runs in the woods, the animal deer.

Mrs. Danoff: You're right. How about *end* and *and*?

Lizzie: *E-n-d* is the end of a story or something. *A-n-d* means both things together.

Mrs. Danoff: That's well said, Lizzie. It's also Pick-a-Friend Friday so who would you like to choose?

Lizzie: Danielle.

Danielle comes up and circles We've.

Danielle: I circled *we've* because the other one means to *weave* a blanket or something. Anne.

Anne comes up and circles week.

Anne: Do I get to do the punctuation, too?

Mrs. Danoff: You can give someone else that turn. Tell us about *week* and *weak*.

Anne: *W-e-a-k* is when you don't feel good like you're weak after being sick.

Mrs. Danoff: That's right. Well said!

Anne: I pick Emily!

Emily: It's not a question, so I'll circle the period.

The letter continues in this way, with children circling the correct word or punctuation and explaining their choices.

Extension Activities

✳ Begin or add to a list of homonyms.

✳ Invite children to read sentences using different kinds of expression like anger, sadness, happiness, or questioning. Ask which would be the appropriate punctuation.

◀ *Fickle Fridays can be fun for exploring homophones.*

Special Days

Some days, no matter where in the week they fall, are special because they are holidays. These might include Halloween, the 100th Day, Valentine's Day, or any day you wish to make special, like Hat Day. You can cut a piece of chart paper into an appropriate shape to make these letters extra fun. Just take a piece off the pad, fold it in half, draw your shape, and then cut. (See illustration on page 58.) That is how I cut the rabbit coming out of the hat and the heart at right and below. For the 100, I just drew the form and then cut around it. The children absolutely love letters written on shapes.

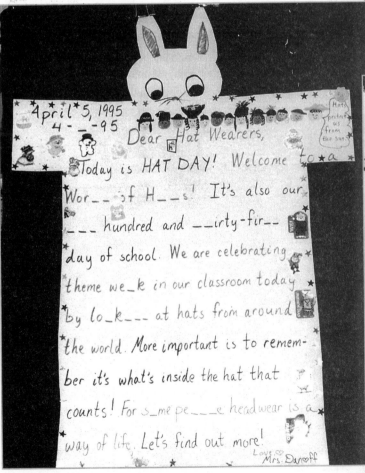

Fun shapes can make days special. Follow the directions on page 58 for easy steps to great designs.

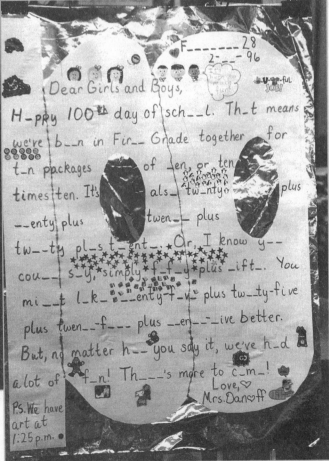

It's easy to create special shapes to celebrate a holiday or tie into a theme. Simply fold a piece of chart paper in half and draw half a shape, as shown below. Then cut out the shape and unfold. Now you're ready to write your letter!

Hat Day

A letter can be the very thing to launch a theme or get a special activity going. One year we decided to celebrate spring with a new spring hat, inviting children to bring in and show off their favorite hat or to tell about a special hat in their family. Then students created their own hat out of construction paper and wrote about why it was special to them. I dedicated the whole day to the idea of hats. Children from various cultures brought in traditional dress and talked about it.

I like to prepare children for this special day by reading aloud from some exceptional literature. Books that work well with this theme include *Aunt Flossie's Hats and Crabcakes Later* by Elizabeth Fitzgerald (Clarion, 1991), *Hats, Hats, Hats,* by Anne Morris (William Morrow, 1989), *Chicken Sunday* by Patricia Polacco (The Putnam Grosset Group, 1989), *Ho for a Hat!* by William Jay Smith (Little Brown, 1964), *Jennie's Hat* by Ezra Jack Keats (Harper & Row, 1966), and *Uncle Nacho's Hat* adapted by Harriet Rohmer (Children's Book Press, 1989).

▲ *Students design and write about their own hats for Hat Day.*

Skills

✳ learning about different cultures

✳ writing

✳ verbal expression

Extension Activities

✳ Cut out a huge hat from a large roll of paper. Give children lots of craft items with which to decorate it.

✳ Help children make individual paper hats. Encourage them to incorporate many design qualities, and then have them write a descriptive piece about their hat.

✳ Research hats from different cultures and provide lots of books and filmstrips about hats. Collect a variety of hats, and invite each child to choose one kind of hat—from a book, filmstrip, or your collection— and become an expert on it. Then children can write about their hats— who wears them, what they're made of, etc.

Fun with 100th Day

Pictured below are two more 100th Day letters. You can see how the letters can get the festivities going.

Skills

✳ counting by skips

✳ place value

Extension Activity

Count by skips and celebrate the 100th Day by counting things all day. Have each child bring in a collection of 100 things to display. Then break into groups to count in all the different ways, i.e., by 2s, 5s, 10s.

100th Day is fun for all! ▶

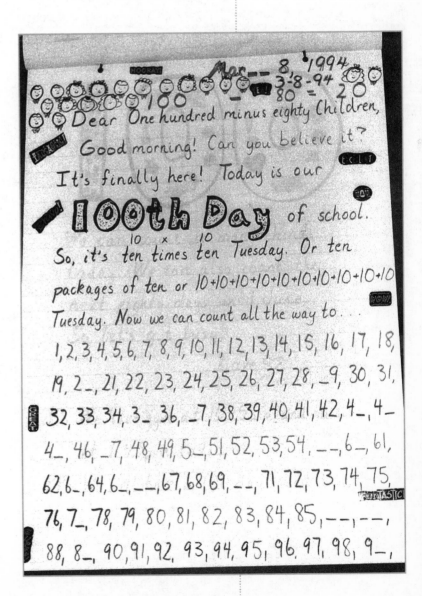

Valentines

The Valentine Letter from February 14, 2000, was simply read and enjoyed by the whole class. After reading it, I began a discussion that went something like this:

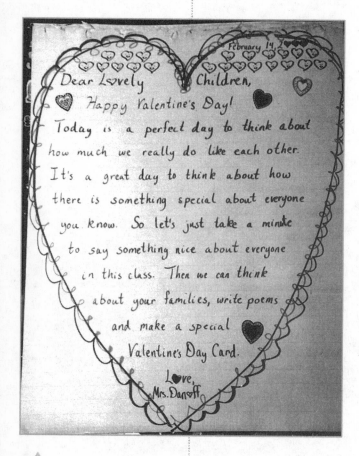

Dear Lovely Children,

Happy Valentine's Day!

Today is a perfect day to think about how much we really do like each other. It's a great day to think about how there is something special about everyone you know. So let's just take a minute to say something nice about everyone in this class. Then we can think about your families, write poems and make a special Valentine's Day Card.

Love,
Mrs. Danoff

The Valentine's Day letter encouraged us all to take a minute and appreciate everyone in our class.

Mrs. Danoff: I'll begin by saying how much I enjoy teaching everyone in this class. You all work so well together like a real little community. I hear you being helpful and saying nice things to each other all the time. It's a pleasure to be here with you. [Hands shot up immediately, wanting to join in.] Kathy.

Kathy: Cyrus is funny.

Cyrus: Kathy is very smart.

Anne: Lizzie is always a good friend to me.

Alison: Emily always cares about how I feel.

Noah: Zander is a great artist!

Christian: Alex draws good trucks.

Alex: Christian draws great trucks!

Danielle: Stephanie can spell just about any word.

This went on and on with agreement in between. Then:

Mrs. Danoff: Let's see now if you can think of some nice things to say about each of your family members. We can write two-words-to-a-line poems for Valentine's Day. For instance, here's mine:

> My family
> My sons
> Happy Josh
> Cheery Zac
> My husband
> Tall Saul
> I love
> Them all
> Very Much!

Extension Activity

Have the children write poems and make valentines for their families.

*N*o matter what day of the week it is, the Daily Letter can get it off to a great start. The next chapter describes how you can use the Daily Letter as a model for journal writing.

CHAPTER 5

Journal Writing

The last chapter demonstrated how you can teach and reinforce a variety of literacy and math skills while writing on just about any topic in the Daily Letter. In addition, you're modeling letter-writing conventions every day—the use of the date, the salutation, the closing. But the letter is more than that. I think of it as my journal entry for the day, and as such, it serves as a wonderful model for my students when they write their own journal entries.

Journal writing encompasses a wide range of writing forms. In my journal entries, I include detailed descriptions of places and things, sometimes even drawing a diagram to illustrate what I'm writing about. I might record directions on how to do something that I've recently learned, or I might write a story about what happened over the weekend. So in the course of writing my Daily Letter, I can model description, process-writing, narrative, and much more.

In thinking about the letter as a journal entry, I'm struck by how well this format works as a classroom management tool, providing kids with an outlet for their pent-up excitement about an event or preparing them for the week ahead, as a way of strengthening the home-school connection (by keeping parents informed of what's going on at school), and as a vehicle for modeling how to generate and organize ideas. It provides a plethora of opportunities for teaching! This chapter will highlight just a few of the ways I use the Daily Letter as a model journal entry.

A Student's Space

What makes journal writing very special in my classroom is that I do not write in children's journals. It is their platform. I want children to have at least one place where teacher correction is not an issue. If I do want to make a comment or suggestion or note a mistake that's repeated over several weeks, I place a small sticky note or highlighting tape on the page, both of which can be removed.

As I get to know children better, I do use a sticky note to write a word correctly that is repeatedly misspelled. Once I do this, children often begin asking me to write more correctly spelled words on sticky notes, and I do. For a struggling writer, I have even used the 4″ x 6″ lined sticky notes and had the child dictate what he or she wants to write. I write it and then the child can copy it into his or her journal.

Preparing for the Week Ahead with Journals

Children often arrive at school on Monday mornings full of stories and energy from their weekend activities and family adventures. Whether it's a birthday party, a trip to the zoo, or a walk in the park, children want to tell you—and each other—all about it. To get kids started, I write my Daily Letter about my weekend (at right).

I like this activity because it helps children recall events as well. From time to time I hear them say that they have forgotten what they did over the weekend. I have suggested to parents that they discuss the weekend's events Sunday evening or Monday morning to help their children's recall ability.

A typical Monday letter that talks about my weekend.

Skills

※ vocabulary development

※ writing and recall of events

※ spelling

Sample Lesson

You'll notice that I omitted letters from certain vocabulary words, challenging students to recall and spell them. Also, you'll see that we worked on a spelling pattern. Did I plan that? Well, I knew that *rice* and *slice* rhyme and have the same rime (spelling pattern); the kids picked up on this and took off with more rhyming words in that family. And all of this teaching occurred in a letter that modeled the kind of writing I wanted my children to do. Talking about my weekend naturally led to conversations about what they did, so it served as a useful pre-writing activity as well. Part of our conversation follows.

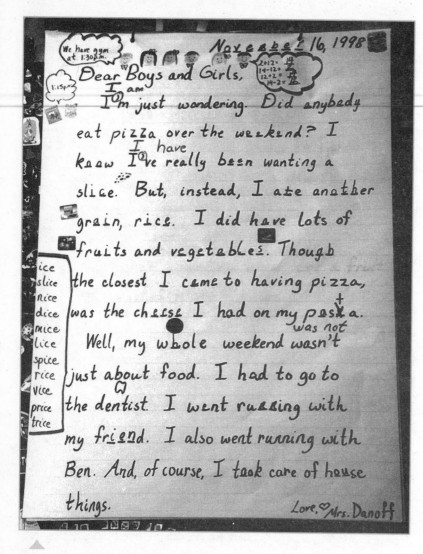

Here's the same letter but filled in with the children's responses. Notice the rhyming word list they generated on the side of the chart.

Mrs. Danoff: Jeffrey, will you read the next sentence please.

Jeffrey: [Reading] *I've really been wanting a slice.* Yeah, I had pizza Friday night. My whole family was having it. Now you're making me hungry for it again.

Mrs. Danoff: Me too! Dana, read the next sentence please.

Dana: [Reading] *But, instead, I ate another gr—* Oh that's *grain*! *But, instead, I ate another grain, r—* Is that *rice*? Because I just realized that rhymes with *slice*!

Mrs. Danoff: Yes, you're right, Dana.

And before I could even say anything else, because children love rhymes …

Emily: How about *ice*?

Allison: I know, *nice*!

Victoria: *Dice*!

Mrs. Danoff: Okay, I'll start a list going down the side.

We continue with the letter, fill in the words and have short discussions.

Mrs. Danoff: Raise your hand if you did eat pizza this weekend. [Class responds.] Raise your hand if you had to go to the dentist this weekend, like I did. [Class responds.] Oh, Emily you had to go to the dentist too?

Emily: Yes, and I can't wait to write about it in my weekend notes. Because look, I finally lost a tooth. And the dentist had to pull it out. Can I have a tooth sticker now?

Mrs. Danoff: That's exciting news! Your first tooth! Sure, go take a sticker. Then let's write our weekend notes . Yes, Andres, you look like you're bursting to tell us something.

Andres: My aunt came to visit from Paraguay this weekend and she brought so many things with her. I can hardly wait to write about that!

Mrs. Danoff: That is exciting! Well, let's start writing right now so we can hear about all this exciting news.

This letter allowed me to review my weekend activities, tie them into the current theme, and prepare kids for another week at school. At the same time, we reviewed vocabulary and reinforced a spelling pattern. Not bad for 9 A.M. on a Monday morning!

More Monday Letters

Not all Monday letters fit so nicely into the curriculum—but they all have a teaching purpose. Take a look at the following letters to see how I taught organization and description in the context of Monday letters.

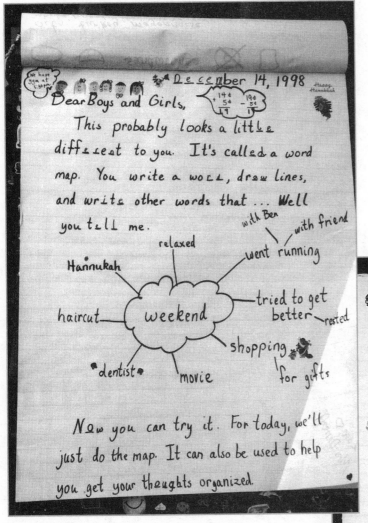

I used a word map one Monday to review weekend events and introduce a new way to organize ideas. Then I encouraged children to try it when they wrote their own journal entries. Even kindergartners can draw a word map. The teacher can write one key word and have the children draw their weekend experiences.

In this letter, I wrote about my weekend, which include a birthday party, an event all my kids can relate to. I also wanted to focus on describing words, so I included several, and we circled them after reading the letter. The children's writing that day was indeed more descriptive.

December 14, 1998

Dear Boys and Girls,

This probably looks a little different to you. It's called a word map. You write a word, draw lines, and write other words that ... Well you tell me.

relaxed
Hannukah
haircut — weekend
dentist
movie
with Ben
with friend
went running
tried to get better — rested
shopping for gifts

Now you can try it. For today, we'll just do the map. It can also be used to help you get your thoughts organized.

J———— ——, 1999

Dear Boys and Girls,

You kn__ h_w you always t_l_ me about b__th__y part___? This past w__k__d, I actually w_nt to a birthday party. But it wasn't for a ch___. It was for a fr___ who is n__ ½ a century old, or 50 years "young." Th_r_ was so much delic____ food. My faro____ part of di____ was the garlic mash__ potat___. That was topp__ by the rich and cr___y ch____te c_k_ for de__ert. Of course, it was so fabulous to see our friend happily surprised.

Lore,
Mrs. Danoff

The Friday Journal

The home-school connection is especially important with young children. One way I've found to keep families informed about what's going on at school is by having students write a journal entry on Fridays that sums up the week. This activity provides a sense of closure for them and opens up communication with parents about school activities. One friend called it the "nothing" letter, referring to children's common response when asked what they did in school that day; the journal provides a place to record all those "nothings" that can then be shared with parents.

Even kindergartners can participate in this kind of journal writing. They can write one or two words and then draw pictures to illustrate the week's events. As the months go by, their growth in reading and writing will be reflected in their journal entries. By the end of the year, some kindergartners can compose a sentence or two.

A letter summing up the week's activities reinforces and reviews the learning that took place, generating plenty of thoughts for a journal entry. The letter at left is an example of such a letter; it sparked a lively discussion of the week's events and motivated students to capture their own thoughts in their journal. Friday letters begin as simple as this one, from a first week in November. They can progress to include an extra skill such as Fickle Friday letters which work on homonyms (see Chapter 4).

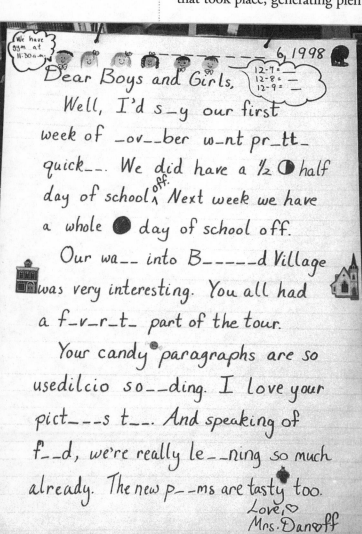

This Friday letter summarized our week, helping kids remember events to write home about.

Skills

✳ recalling events

✳ written and verbal expression

✳ sequencing of events

✳ reinforcing and reviewing learning

✳ organizing thoughts

Sample Lesson

In addition to wrapping up the week and getting kids ready to write their own journal entries, this particular letter also begins to introduce fractions.

Mrs. Danoff: Read the letter to yourselves. As you get to your favorite thing that we did this week, raise your hand. Then keep reading. Remember, thumbs up when you're finished reading.

Allow time for children to read independently, about five minutes.

Mrs. Danoff: Sarah will you read the first sentence?

Sarah: [Reading] *Well, I'd say our first week of November went pretty quickly.*

Mrs. Danoff: Was that anyone's favorite part of the week?

Jed: That's not really telling a part of the week yet!

Mrs. Danoff: You're right, Jed. Read the next sentence for us.

Jed: [Reading] *We did have a half day of school off.* That was my favorite part because I got to go into the city.

Ellen: Not me. I had to go to the dentist.

Mrs. Danoff: Raise your hand if the half day was your favorite part of the week. Why do you think I shaded in part of that circle?

Harpal: Because it's a half?

Mrs. Danoff: Yes! Good for you! Kelly please read the next sentence.

Kelly: [Reading] *Next week we have a whole day of school off.*

Mrs. Danoff: That's the end of the first paragraph. Who can tell me what the first paragraph was about?

Kelly: About days off from school.

Mrs. Danoff: Good for you! Sam please read the next sentence.

Sam: Oh, I really wanted to read that sentence 'cause that was my favorite part of the week. [Reading] *Our walk into Bedford Village was very interesting.* I know it's not until the next sentence, but can I tell my favorite part of the walk?

Mrs. Danoff: You asked so nicely—sure!

Sam: I just loved going into the court house. The judge's bench was so cool!

Mrs. Danoff: I'm glad you found that so interesting, Sam. Who can read the sentence that asks about your favorite part of the tour?

Elijah: [When called upon] I can. But then can I tell mine?

Mrs. Danoff: Sure.

Elijah: [Reading] *You all had a favorite part of the tour.* The graveyard was definitely the coolest! I especially liked when we had to find the grave of the three kids that died in the fire. I even remember the year was 1783.

Mrs. Danoff: Well, good for you! You can include that detail in your journal this week. Let's go on to the next paragraph. Would someone like to read that whole paragraph? [Many hands go up.] Give it a try, Kara.

Kara: [Reading] *Your candy p -r - par -a gr-a…* I forget how does *gh* go? Is it silent?

Mrs. Danoff: In this word *gh* sound like "f," fuh. Good for you!

Kara: Okay then, *paragraphs.* Oh, that's what you just said I could read. [Continues reading] *usedilcio.* Oh, that's the funny Friday word.

Anne:	It's delicious!
Kara:	[Continues reading] I really did like learning about food. It is so much fun. But I never had a teacher let me eat candy for writing before!
Mrs. Danoff:	I'm sure your parents would enjoy hearing about that, too! Who can tell me something we learned about food this week?
Krystal:	Well, I already knew it tastes good! But I really liked finding out that pizza has fruit in it!
Charles:	Yeah! That's funny. I bet my dad doesn't even know that!
Mrs. Danoff:	Wow! You've remembered so many things about food.

I continue bringing out more detail for discussion, and children fill in the blanks and do the math problems at the top of the page.

Mrs. Danoff:	Raise your hand and tell me a word you want to use in your writing today.
Elijah:	I'm going to use the word "favorite" to tell about the graveyard! I really liked that!
Sarah:	Well, I want to make sure I spell *Bedford Village* right because we live there.

More children respond.

Mrs. Danoff:	Good for all of you! Let's take out our writing journals now. See if you can use the word *delicious* in your paragraphs to your parents. But remember to spell it correctly!

This letter illustrates how you can integrate Fickle Friday and reviewing the week's events in preparation for a journal entry.

Word Maps

You can also use a word map for a Friday letter, enlisting the children's help in naming the week's activities. It's an appealing alternative on a morning when you're running late, and it lets you reinforce this means of organizing ideas.

Skill

✳ using a word map to generate ideas to begin writing

Sample Lesson

Zander: I love that big heart you drew. I guess we're getting ready for Valentine's Day.

Mrs. Danoff: Yes, well, I thought it would get us in the mood.

Danielle: It's pretty. I like it.

Mrs. Danoff: Me, too. I love Valentine's Day. This letter looks kind of empty though. I'll need all of you to help me fill it up.

The children volunteer information about the week. I demonstrate by writing it down.

Alison: Can we write about the week in our journals that way, too?

Mrs. Danoff: Sure. But be sure to choose your favorite thing and write a few sentences about that, too. Writing a word map is supposed to give you ideas from which you then write your whole story. For today, we'll just try it this way.

The class is pleased and excited to try their hand at drawing a word map in the shape of a heart, but there are other ideas too.

Evan: Can I make mine look like something else? I really want to draw a groundhog.

Mrs. Danoff: If you can do it, go ahead. A word map can be shaped like anything you like, whatever reminds you of your subject. Certainly this week began with a bitter cold and disappointing groundhog day. I know I was hoping for an early spring.

Extension Activity

Invite children to turn their word maps into weekly journal entries to take home and share with parents.

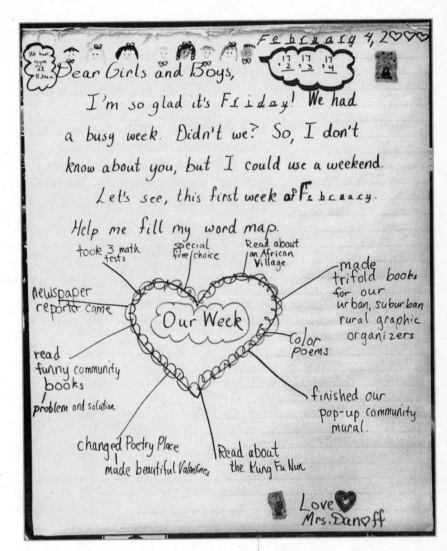

A word map on a Friday teaches an effective way to brainstorm information for writing.

Vacation Notes

When children are away from school for more than a few days, I find it helpful to write Vacation Notes. This process helps them recall and share important events and serves as a transition back into the school environment. To ensure success, I encourage students to write a list of activities they plan to do over vacation before they leave. Then, when they return, they can consult their list to stimulate their memories. I model both the list-making and the vacation-notes-writing process in Daily Letters.

We have gym at 1:30pm.

____ 30, 1998

Dear Boys and Girls,

It was a l-o-n-g weekend!

The q_est___ sh___dn't be, "What did I do over the w__k__d?" Rather, "What didn't I do over the weekend?" Because, I did so much! And, it all began and end__ with food shopping! Of course, family was an important part of my weekend t___

I began by making stuffing, cole slaw and cranberry sau_e with my son's help. Then we went to my sister's h__se for Th_____giving dinner. It's so wonderful to sit ar_____ a table and see everybody. But bef____ we all kn__ it, dinner was done, de__ert was served and it was t_m_ to say goodb____. That

This letter provides an example of vacation notes I wrote after the Thanksgiving holiday.

felt sad.

After Th___day I was busy c___king some more, because my son and his girlfr___d were always hungry for br__kfast and dinner. I just love having them home. My other son had to go back to Vermont earlier.

Anyway, in between food shop____ and cooking I w_nt run_____, I read, I wrote, I cleaned. I also had pl__ty of time to relax.

How about you? Can you remember your Th____g_____ Holiday?

Love,
Mrs. Danoff

This chapter has provided examples of how you can use the letter to facilitate journal writing on Monday and Friday, but you can adapt this for any day of the week. While the Daily Letter is certainly a natural model for journal and letter writing, it lends itself well to other kinds of writing, too. The next chapter gives examples of how to use the letter for descriptive, poetry, and research writing.

Descriptive, Poetry, and Research Writing

The last chapter demonstrated how to use the Daily Letter to model journal writing. You can also use it to model descriptive writing, poetry writing, and even research writing. The subject of the letter can review the content you want your students to write about, and the letter itself can be a model of the kind of writing you want students to do.

Descriptive Writing

I like to work with descriptive writing early in the year. I've found I can harness the energy and excitement Halloween arouses by inviting kids to bring in a piece of their favorite candy the day after Halloween. I then use the candy as a prop for a lesson on descriptive writing. It works well because kids are motivated to write about their candy, and this particular prop allows them to explore details from all five senses.

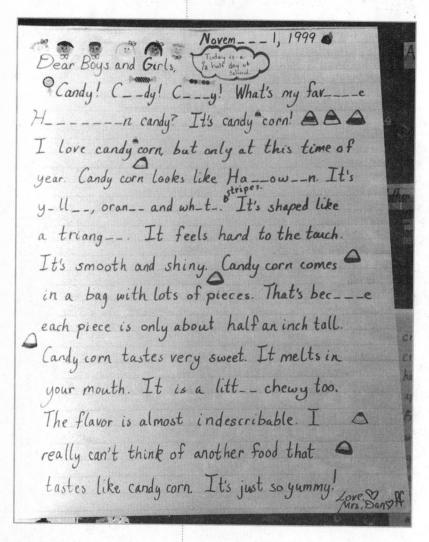

A fun Halloween letter introduced descriptive writing.

Skills

✳ discussing sensory detail
✳ descriptive paragraph writing

Sample Lesson

Zander: Mrs. Danoff, you really must like candy corn.

Noah: You draw it so well.

Carly: I'm getting hungry for some right now.

Mrs. Danoff: You've had no problem guessing my favorite candy!

Emily: I didn't even need to read the letter, it's all over it! Are you going to guess ours?

Mrs. Danoff: Actually I'm hoping you'll do such a great job writing about your favorite candy that it won't be hard for me to guess.

Carly: Oh, so that's why we got to bring candy to school today.

Mrs. Danoff: There's always something special going on in here! Alex, you're the helper today; will you read the first line?

Students read the letter and fill in the words.

Mrs. Danoff: Tell me the types of things that made my candy description so "yummy," as Danielle said.

Danielle: You said what it looks like.

Mrs. Danoff: Can you read that sentence for us please, Danielle?

Danielle: [Reading] *Candy corn looks like Halloween.*

Mrs. Danoff: Good, is there another sentence that tells what it looks like?

Lizzie: You said it's yellow, orange, and white. You also said it's shaped like a triangle. Do you want me to read those sentences?

Mrs. Danoff: No, that's fine, Lizzie. Does anybody see what else I told about the candy?

Anne: There's another sentence that tells what it looks like if its size has to do with that.

Mrs. Danoff: Good for you, Anne. Of course it does! Read that sentence for us.

Anne: [Reading] *That's because each piece is only about half an inch tall.* Oh, but I see another sentence about what it looks like.

Mrs. Danoff: Let's see if your friend Alison can find that sentence.

Alison: Is it the sentence that says candy corn is shiny?

Mrs. Danoff: That's right, Alison. What does smooth describe though? Greg?

Greg: That's what it feels like.

Mrs. Danoff: Good for you!

We continue this way until the five senses are brought out.

Mrs. Danoff: We've spoken about the five…

Class: Senses!

Mrs. Danoff: [Flipping to new chart page] Okay, so tell me what they are again.

Writes them down as shown.

Mrs. Danoff: Let's come up with some words that you can use to write your own paragraphs describing your favorite candy.

Greg: Can we use some of your words?

Mrs. Danoff: Of course. Let's start with some of those.

Cyrus: But my candy is chocolate on the inside so it won't be orange.

Mrs. Danoff: That's a good word, *inside*. Where could that go? And what does orange describe?

Cyrus: Orange is a color, so that's what it looks like.

Mrs. Danoff: That's right!

The class continues to add words to the list.

Carly: All this is making me hungry. Can we eat our candy now?

Mrs. Danoff: Not until you write your paragraphs and get up to the part about what it tastes like. But be careful opening it; you'll need your wrapper for your picture. Oh, and remember, if you want to really see what your candy is made out of where could you find that?

Students brainstormed this list of descriptive words for each of the five senses. They then consulted this list when writing their own descriptive paragraphs.

Describing

sight
color(s), shades
shiny
shape
size
beautiful
pattern
pointy
round
square
rectangle
triangle
log
circles

taste
inside
outside
ingredients
delicious
extrodinary
hot, cold
sugary
flavor
wonderful
sour, sweet
salty
spicy
chocolate, vanilla
caramel
peanut, nutty
sticky

touch
bumpy
smooth
texture
chewy
liquidy
mushy
flexible
gooey
sticky
creamy

smell
sweet
chocolate
caramel

hear
crunchy
soft
smooth

sensation
yummy
tasty
delicious
supremo
wonderful
delightful

Christian: You mean on the wrapper. Mine has words I can't even say!

Anne: Mine too! But it does say *chocolate* here!

Noah: You mean we get to eat our candy in school before lunch?

Mrs. Danoff: Only on this day. Remember, it's a half day, too. Ready to write now?

Zander: I can hardly wait. This sounds like fun!

Extension Activity

Children write a paragraph describing their candy using their five senses. Then they draw a picture of themselves in their Halloween costumes. Glue the edited paragraph and the candy wrapper next to the picture.

▲ *A student's descriptive paragraph about her favorite Halloween candy.*

My Favorite Candy

My favorite candy is a Milky Way. They are very yummy. The size is two inches. It is bumpy. It's a little chewy too. It smells like chocolate to me. It looks like a log. The caramel is good. It is hard. It is very good. It very chocolate. The caramel jumps out. I can taste the caramel when I take a bite. It's very yummy.

by Courtney

Poetry Writing

Poetry writing can be a joy for children from kindergarten on up. Children appreciate the freedom and flexibility this kind of writing gives them, as opposed to more formal narrative or research writing, which demands complete sentences and strict adherence to punctuation conventions.

Pattern Poems

You can use the same teaching techniques demonstrated in the descriptive writing section to introduce poetry writing. In the letter shown at right, I write about different kinds of foods we've been talking about in our unit on food. I omitted letters from several adjectives, and we discussed these kinds of words as we filled in the blanks. Then, on another piece of chart paper, we brainstormed more words to describe food and ways we can serve food. From these charts, students had all the words they needed to write a pattern poem about food.

I introduced the format of the pattern poem on another piece of chart paper, shown at right. Working from these charts, which remained posted at the front of the room, children wrote their very own pattern poems. The letter, follow-up discussion, and charts provided the scaffolding they needed to compose their first poem of the year, and helped them think more about our theme unit. You can adapt this activity to just about any theme.

I introduced the format of the pattern poem on a piece of chart paper. ▶

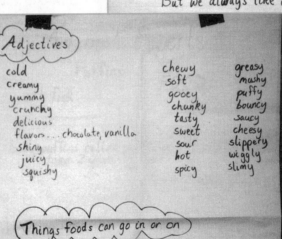

Dear El_v__ plus El____ Children,
This morning I am really thinking about all the d_l_c_o_s f__d we all lik to eat. S_m_ of it is juicy. Some of it is cr___m_. Some foods are cr___c_y Still, other foods are sti___y. I'm s_r_ you've had foods that are fl_ffy t__.
Now, it's very interesting that we like some f__ds h_t. While we like s_m_ foods c__d. Wh_ we even eat some foods h_t or cold. W__m can be good t__.
Let's rem_m__r that we eat some foods on a pl__e. Others are serv__ in a b__l. But we always like all foods in our m__th.
Love, Mrs. Danoff

This letter introduced adjectives used to describe foods, which set up a pattern-poetry lesson on that topic.

◀ *We brainstormed adjectives and nouns that could be used in our food pattern poems.*

provided the scaffolding they needed to compose their first poem of the year, and helped them think more about our theme unit. You can adapt this activity to just about any theme.

Skill

✳ writing a pattern poem using describing words

Extension Activity

Have children write pattern poems about food. Then have them use construction paper to make a picture of the food on which to glue their edited copy.

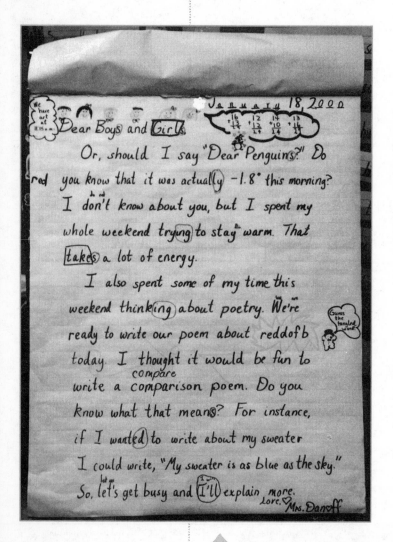

This letter set up our study of comparison poems.

Comparison Poems

You can also use the Daily Letter to introduce other types of poetry; the one dated January 18, 2000, shows how I introduced comparison poems. We worked on root words, word endings, and contractions as we filled in the blanks; then we discussed *compare,* which was one of our vocabulary words. This discussion was a natural lead-in to the comparison poems I wanted to write for our communities unit.

Skill

✳ understanding comparing

Extension Activity

Choose a subject and write comparison poems, for example, about your home town:

> Bedford is as green as all the oak trees.
> Bedford is as quiet as a bunny.
> Bedford is as brown as the earth.
> Bedford is as loud as one dog barking.
> Bedford is as blue as the spring sky.
> Bedford is as warm as my home.

Cinquains

Another way to use the letter to jumpstart poetry writing is illustrated in the letter excerpted on page 78. It was a Monday letter, so the first part told about my weekend. The second part addressed our current unit—urban communities—and introduced a poetry term—*cinquain*. Since cinquains require careful attention to syllabication, we then used the letter to practice breaking words into syllables.

Here's an excerpt from the poetry part of our letter reading:

Skills

✳ syllabification

✳ counting

✳ dictionary skills

Sample Lesson

After reading the letter, there was some interested discussion about my taking a test over the weekend. Then:

Mrs. Danoff: Who can tell me what the first paragraph of my letter is about?

Danielle: It's about your weekend, and the test you took.

Mrs. Danoff: What is the second paragraph about?

Carly: That we're going to write a *kuh* …

Mrs. Danoff: That's a soft *c* in front of an *i*. Keep trying.

Carly: Oh, okay then it's *cin*?

Mrs. Danoff: Yes, go on.

Carly: *Cin qu*

Mrs. Danoff: *a-i* together, so which vowel is talking?

Carly: The *a* so it's *cinquain*?

Mrs. Danoff: Great! Let's all try that together now. *Cinquain*.

Children: *Cinquain*! What's that?

Mrs. Danoff: Raise your hand if you can read the sentence that gives a clue.

Rachel: [Reading] *If you think about languages you may have heard, think about counting.* But I'm not sure what you mean.

Zander: She means have you counted in other languages. Yes, I have, because I went to Greece last summer and it was so much fun!

Noah: Well, I can count in Japanese because I'm half Japanese.

Alison: My friend, Amalia is from Mexico, so I can count in Spanish.

Several Children: I can count in Spanish too! Uno, dos, tres, quatro, cinco, sies …

Mrs. Danoff: Okay, stop with *cinco*. What does *cinco* mean?

Alison: It means five. Oh, I get it. A cinquain has five of something?

Mrs. Danoff: Yes, it has five lines. And, each line has a certain number of syllables. You all remember what a syllable is, don't you? Raise your hand if you can tell me.

Kathy: It's where you can break a word if it doesn't fit on a line.

Lizzie:	You can clap a syllable.
Anne:	It helps you sound out a word.
Mrs. Danoff:	You're all right. Just to review, let's try a few claps with our names. [After clapping names] Sometimes it is hard to decide where a syllable is in a word. What do you think can help with that?
Christian:	Maybe the dictionary, because it has words in it?
Mrs. Danoff:	That's right! Go get one Christian, in case we need to check. We're going to go through some of the words in the letter now and make slash lines where the syllables are. That will help us write cinquains, because each line of a cinquain has to have a different number of syllables.

Sa t/ur/day morning. I'm stu/dy/ing about pe o/ple who speak two lan/gua/ges. As part of my study, I needed to be tested in English. I had to listen to taped con/ver/sa/ti o n s and answer ques/t i o n s about what the pe o/ple were saying. I had to be a ver/y good lis/ten/er!

I was also think/ing about our po/e/try writing over the week/end. For our ur/b a n poem we can learn how to wr_t_ a cinquain. If you

After we read the letter, we practiced breaking words into syllables in preparation for writing cinquains.

Extension Activity

Use the letter as a class to syllabify some words. Then, give each child a turn. You can see from the close-up that some mistakes were made and corrected with class or dictionary help.

Write cinquains about a subject you are studying.

> LINE 1 (2 SYLLABLES): states the title
> LINE 2 (4 SYLLABLES): describes the title
> LINE 3 (6 SYLLABLES): expresses an action
> LINE 4 (8 SYLLABLES): expresses a feeling
> LINE 5 (2 SYLLABLES): another word for the title

Here's one the class wrote together for our urban unit:

City
Busy Island
Hurry everywhere
People, cars, buses, subway trains
Urban

Interactive Stories

In addition to introducing all sorts of poetry writing, you can also use the letter to tell an interactive story. That is, the teacher begins a story, encourages children to give feedback, and then incorporates that feedback the next day in the following letter. The children can then view an ongoing model of how to develop their own stories and hear how a writer makes choices when telling a story. The three letters pictured here demonstrate this kind of sequence. We were writing what I call "small tales." These are stories based on my tales about little people. I integrated story writing with a math unit on measurement.

Skills

✳ story writing and storytelling

✳ sequencing events

✳ incorporating a beginning, middle, and end

✳ quotes

✳ descriptive detail

March __, 1999

Dear F__e times F__r Ch_____,

Well, let's see now... Yesterday, in my small tale, I was only 5__ tall. After I'd g_n_ for a sw__ in a tulip, I decid__ I wanted to be a little taller. That's be_____ of what happened with the hummingb__d.

A b__uti___ ruby throated hummingbird tried to __ink the d__ in the br___t y____w tulip. When it saw me in th___. As you can imagine, we both got really scared! It was at that frightening moment that I decided to wish upon a st__ ag__n. I wish__ to be 10 cm taller. So, how tall did I become?
Love, Mrs. Danoff

March 5, 1999

27 + 54   54 - 27

Dear Girls and Boys,

You may r_m_m_e_, from y____day. that I gr__ to be __cm. tall. Well, since I was still in___e that br____ y____w tulip, it broke. I came cra__ing do__ to the gr___d with a l__d and n__sy thud. I landed in the cr___y oozy, thick brown e__th.

I guess I disturbed the f_t gr__n h__gry c_t__pill__ who was looking for his lunch. He gazed at me and shouted, "You don't belong in this garden!" It was at that very moment that I realized I could h__r animals talk now.
What do you think I replied?
Love, Mrs. Danoff

March 9, 1999

77 + 19   96 - 19

Dear Girls and Boys,

So, th__e I was, standing in my g_r_n, with all those extrodinary creat__es surr___ding me. Each one of them had an exc_ll__t suggest___ as to what my job c___d be in the garden.

"Trim the fl____s," fluttered the butterfl__
"Use the d__ to water the garden," buzzed all the bees.
"Help us keep air in the e__th," suggested the pink earth worms.
"Keep bigger an__ls out of the garden," squeaked the furry rabbits.

It seemed as if they were all talking at the same t_m_. I lis__n__ with gr__t interest. Then, it occurred to me what I really needed to do.
Love, Mrs. Danoff

This series of letters developed an interactive story that served as a model for students' own story writing.

Each day I integrated the children's suggestions from the day before. I was able to incorporate quotes on the March 9 letter—a skill I wanted to review—using the class's suggestions as the suggestions from the animals. I especially liked the sentence, "It seemed as if they were all talking at the same time." That's exactly what happened in my classroom! The children were so excited about this story that they could hardly wait to read the next installment. They even begged me to continue the story by writing a letter while they were at lunch. When the story was finished, the children had seen me work through the writing process, and they had a model story to refer to when writing their own stories.

Extension Activities

* Read from literature some examples of the kind of story you are writing.

* Ask children to tell their own stories.

* Encourage pairs or small groups to write their own story.

Publishing

You can even use the Daily Letter to teach publishing skills. In our school, we have a publishing center—parent volunteers type children's stories and bind them into books. But before children can bring their books to the publishing center, they need to decide how to paginate their stories. I used the letter dated January 10, 2000, to demonstrate how students can indicate page breaks on their copy.

Skill

* paginating a story

Sample Lesson

After reading the letter and filling in the blanks:

Mrs. Danoff: Today you are going to begin taking your rough drafts to the publishing center. You need to paginate your stories. What do you think that means?

Anne: Well it sounds like page, so does it mean to make it into pages?

Mrs. Danoff: Good for you! You have to decide how much writing or text you want on each page. Your book is going to be a picture book. So you'll want to be sure the writing you choose for each page leaves you with an illustration idea. Do you remember the book I read you about what real authors do? (From *Pictures to Words* by Janet Stevens, Holiday House, 1995, or *What Do Authors Do?* by Eileen Christelow, Houghton Mifflin, 1995)

Zander: Oh yes, she had to match her pictures and words. That's so cool. Are we going to do that?

Mrs. Danoff: Yes. Let's look at my letter and pretend I am going to make it into a book. I'll use a red marker to make slashes where I want each page to end. You all help me to decide. Just like the author in the book, I'll draw little boxes with possible picture ideas. Where do you think the first slash or the first page should end?

Thomas: I think it should end with "read on," because that's sort of… Well, the next sentence really tells a new thing.

Mrs. Danoff: Okay. What kind of picture could I draw on that page?

Tommy: You could draw yourself being happy. Then on the next page you could draw yourself eating dinner with Mr. Danoff.

Mrs. Danoff: Those are good ideas. Let's see how the rest of the book would unfold.

I used this letter to demonstrate how I would paginate a story in preparation for publication.

Extension Activity

Have the children write stories. Then make the stories into class-published books. Help the children to decide which sentences can go on each page for the purpose of illustrating. For younger children, write a story together as a class. Then copy over the text, divide your class up, and let the children work cooperatively to illustrate each page. They can even work collage style. That is, each child can add a part of the illustration by creating their own. Glue each part to create the final page illustration. (See *The Young Author's Do-It-Yourself Book* by Donna Guthrie, Nancy Bently, and Katy Keck Arnsteen, The Millbrook Press, 1994.)

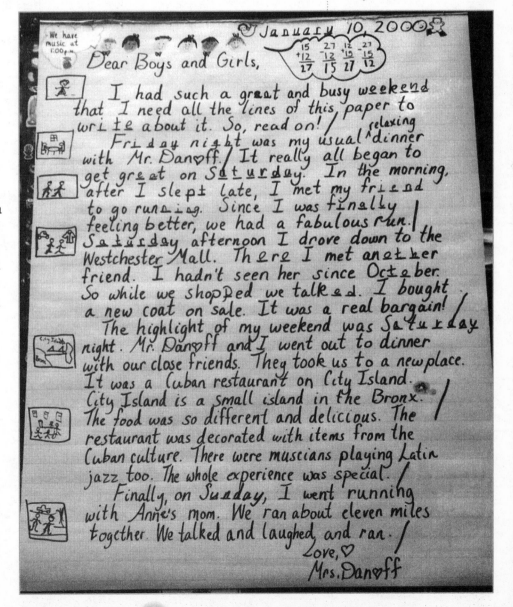

Research Writing

In addition to poetry and story writing, my students practice expository writing in relation to research they do in connection to our theme unit. Once again, I've found the Daily Letter is an excellent platform for modeling this type of writing.

When I wrote the following letter, my class was studying the animals in our community. They gathered information about the animals' habitat, food, offspring, appearance, behavior, and instincts from several sources, including books and the Internet. As the time approached for them to write paragraphs based on their research, I incorporated model paragraphs into the Daily Letter. The letter from March 22, 1999, shows how I wrote about the appearance of a very special animal—me! Then, for homework that week, children wrote paragraphs about themselves in their journals. When it was time to write their research paragraphs, students had seen several models and written on a subject they knew very well.

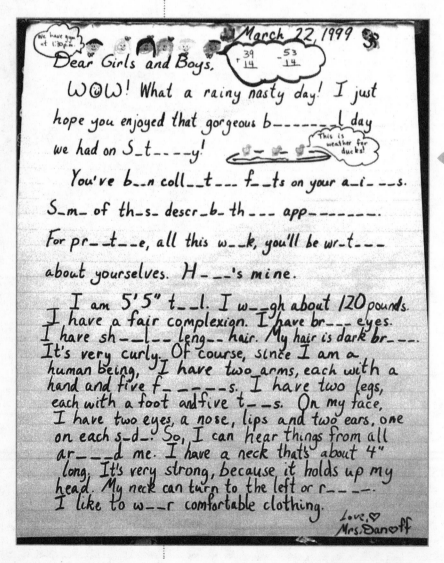

I modeled writing a paragraph about an animal by including the relevant information about myself.

All About My Behavior
Every day I come home after school and have a snack and do my homework. Then I just play. You don't want to know what I do when I'm mad. When I'm happy I smiel. When I'm sad I frown. When I'm exited I get wild. I get wild alot! Sometimes I get anood. I don't get anood that much. But other people do from me. Well that is mostlee what I do.

Chipmunks live in brushy areas in yellow-pine forests. The chipmunk starts the burrow by digging a hole about 25 to 70 cm deep. Chipmunks can also be found living in city parks where there are trees and in areas where it can find protection from the wind and rain. Chipmunks like living in harpwood forestes. When digging a tunnel, the chipmunk uses its teeth to cut roots from trees. The chipmunk also spends time changing its burow. Its burow can be a tunnel and can be 20 feet long. It begins its underground nest by diggen a hole.

Students wrote about their own appearance and behavior in their journals (left). Then they researched an animal found in our community and wrote about its characteristics (right).

Extension Activity

To provide further support, or scaffolding, for your students, model a research paragraph about an animal not found in your community. I wrote about puffins that year; see sample report at right.

My sample paragraph on puffins. ▶

Puffins have a black and white body of feathers. They have a layer of insulating fat. ~~Their wings~~ Their wings, and the neck, top of ~~of~~ their head and tail are black. Their stomach, chests and cheeks are white. Puffins have large gray triangular beaks ~~that are orange and yellow. Their beaks~~ change colors every spring. ~~So the their beak are orange and yellow~~ At that time of year their beaks turn orange and yellow.

~~Puffins have black b~~
Puffins have a black and white body of feathers. They have a layer of insulating fat. Their wings, neck, top of their head and tail are black. Their stomach, chest and cheeks are white. Puffins have large triangular gray beaks that change colors every spring. At that time of year their beaks turn orange and yellow. They have yellow at the corners of their mouth too. Puffins have red rimmed eyes. They have two sets of eyelids. The inner eyelid is transparent. They can see underwater. Puffins have three toed webbed feet that turn orange in the spring. Their bodies are big compared to their wings. So puffins work hard to fly.

While it is almost unavoidable to incorporate every subject you are studying into the Daily Letter, the next chapter shows some specific examples for social studies and science.

Daily Letter
for Social Studies
and Science

The flexibility of the Daily Letter makes it a powerful teaching tool. This chapter demonstrates how you can integrate social studies and science topics into the Daily Letter, so it does double duty—both develops literacy skills and sparks content-area learning.

Social Studies

Social studies themes help students explore and think about their world. It's easy to incorporate social studies topics into daily letters.

Community Living

Pictured below are two Wacky Wednesday letters that integrate our social studies unit: communities. Both before and after correcting the mistakes in these letters, students engaged in lively discussions related to our study of communities. The questions posed in the letter dated January 1999 laid the groundwork for such discussions and for a graphing activity about which kind of community the children would prefer to live in.

Skill

✳ discussion of community issues

Extension Activities

✳ Follow up the discussion by answering the questions.

✳ Conduct a class survey and graph the results.

These letters led directly into a discussion of our social studies unit theme on communities.

▶

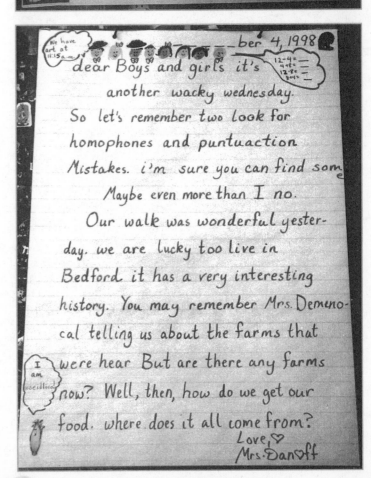

dear Boys and Girls,
we really lerned a lot about an urban community yesterday, it certainly seems like living in a city could be sew much fun. Due you think pepole have more choices in a city? then in a suburban community. do you think ther's less too do in a rural area? wood you rather live in a city write now? What kinds of things make living in a suburb better or worse then in a city? Witch kind of home would you like?

Here's the wacky mystery word

—ber 4, 1998
dear Boys and girls it's another wacky wednesday.
So let's remember two look for homophones and puntuaction Mistakes. i'm sure you can find some Maybe even more than I no.
Our walk was wonderful yesterday. we are lucky too live in Bedford it has a very interesting history. You may remember Mrs. Demunocal telling us about the farms that were hear But are there any farms now? Well, then, how do we get our food. where does it all come from?
Love,
Mrs. Danoff

We have art at 11:15 a.m.

I am possiblical

Changing Times

The letter dated November 17, 1998, led into a discussion about change over time. The questions in the letter began the social studies focus for that day. Seeing a buggy and being able to write about it spontaneously provided motivation for the following discussion; the excitement was difficult to contain.

The questions in this letter got us talking about another social studies topic, changes over time. ▶

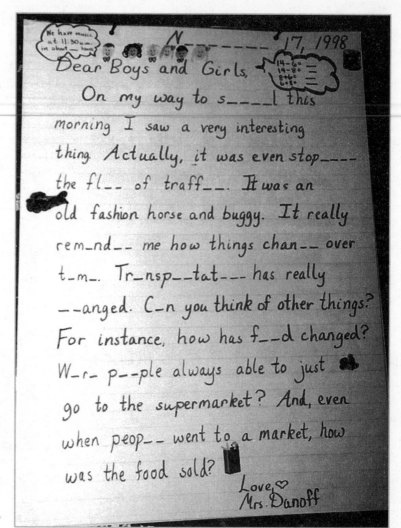

> Dear Boys and Girls,
> On my way to s____l this morning I saw a very interesting thing. Actually, it was even stop_____ the fl__ of traff__. It was an old fashion horse and buggy. It really rem_nd__ me how things chan__ over t_m_. Tr_nsp__tat___ has really __anged. C_n you think of other things? For instance, how has f__d changed? W_r_ p__ple always able to just go to the supermarket? And, even when peop__ went to a market, how was the food sold?
>
> Love,
> Mrs. Danoff

Graham:	Did you really see a horse and buggy this morning? I saw one over the weekend!
Victoria:	Yes, I saw that this morning too. I wonder where it was going.
Andres:	We have one of them on the farm where I live.
Dana:	They're so fun to see.
Jack:	You must have had to drive really slow behind it.
Mrs. Danoff:	Yes, I did, because they sure don't go as fast as a car, do they. Oh, isn't that one change over time?
Graham:	Well, things really do move much faster now! We have jet planes now.
Jack:	We also have really fast trains. Did they have subways then?
Mrs. Danoff:	Well, remember when we looked at the book about New York City. It showed the subways beginning to be built below ground and the horse and buggies above. You know, the people in the horse and buggy this morning were wearing jeans and jackets. What do you think people were wearing when horses and buggies were not unusual sights?

The discussion continued, and the questions in the letter helped us stay focused on our topic.

Food

The letter dated December 15, 1998, celebrated the culmination of our food unit. It also helped to ease the way into trying some new foods at our luncheon and introducing some new vocabulary words, like *flan*.

This letter enabled the children to ask about what some of the foods were. Since children in our class were bringing these foods in, they were able to share their knowledge in a non-threatening way in a familiar environment. I really do think it was this kind of discussion, initiated by the letter, that helped children to try some new foods.

The letter dated November 18, 1997 is an example of how the letter can review concepts learned. When working on the food unit, words like *grain*, *wheat*, *dough*, *kernel*, *stalk*, *vegetables*, and *ground* were also our spelling words. These were reviewed in the letter too.

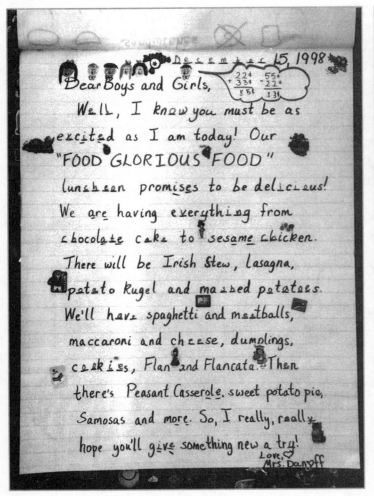

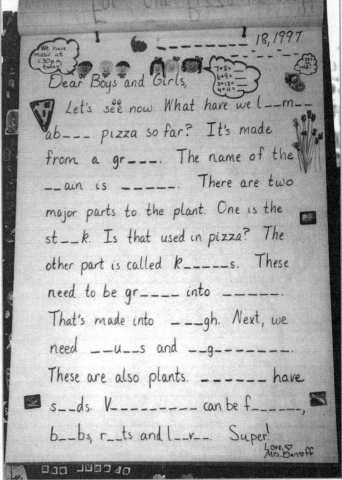

These letters helped us review our food unit.

Dear Boys and Girls, ~~I guess~~   *January 12, 2000*

We have gym at 11:30 a.m. today.

I ~~guess~~ I really stumped you
yesterday with the tangled word,
^{suburban} urbanbsu. But I ^{sure} shore dew
hope you can remember what it
means, especially too you.

    Can you think of ^{some} ~~sum~~ characteristics
^{of} ~~our~~ of ^{our} community? Do we have
subways ^{here} hear? How do most people
get from place twoo place? Are
they're skyscrapers in our community?
Weae do most people live, in what
kinds of homes? Oh, and do you
think a lot of people go too an
urban community to work? Let's sea!

         Love,♥
           Mrs. Danoff

This letter prompted a discussion of suburban communities.

Suburbanhood

Though the letter dated January 12, 2000, was a Wacky Wednesday letter, it led into a very "unwacky" discussion about our suburban community. It helped to set up the ideas needed to complete a graphic organizer that compared our community to an urban community.

Skill

✳ making comparisons

Extension Activity

Have children work on individual or class graphic organizers, like Venn diagrams, to compare the likenesses and differences of areas being studied.

Snow Day

The letter dated January 8, 1999, at right, was a quite an accomplishment. It is always very nerve wracking to be caught in school on the day of a predicted snowstorm because the children are excited and the teachers are nervous about everyone getting home safely. Writing about the subject on everyone's mind gave us all a chance to express our feelings, and it linked nicely to our discussion of community services. If I'd written this letter the day before, it might not have worked so well.

Skill

✳ understanding interdependence within the community, and community workers, rules, and services

Sample Lesson

Mrs. Danoff: So, what do you think? Snow or no snow? Raise your hands and we can take a mini-survey.

Cody: I really think it's going to snow a lot because that's what I heard on the weather report. Is the weather report a community service because it warns us about the weather?

Mrs. Danoff: Yes, you're right. It does do a service for our community. What else do you think will be important if it snows? Mark, your hand is up.

Mark: Well, the snow plows are very important! I'd really like that job. Those trucks are awesome the way they push the snow around.

Deirdre: The bus drivers who take us home will have a very hard job if it snows today. I'm a little worried.

Lissa: Don't worry, because people will have to drive slow. Is that a rule Mrs. Danoff?

Mrs. Danoff: Yes, Lissa, you're right. The speed limit is a rule that will be especially important for people to follow. Now some plows are run by our town, Bedford, but do these plows plow your driveway?

Haley: No, I think my mom pays somebody to do that! Oh, I know, that's a service.

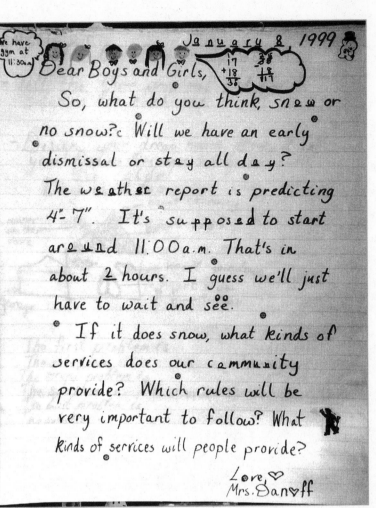

This letter helped vent the excitement and anxiety about a potential snow day, and focused our attention on our social studies unit.

The children were comfortable and their nervous energy was channeled into an intelligent conversation.

Extension Activity

Have the children create a class mural depicting a snowy day. Be sure they include all the community workers needed to make the day safe and fun for them. Then have each child write about the mural and include what they would love to do on a snowy day.

Science

Science is as easy to discuss in the letter as any other subject. I always say science is hard to avoid. It happens every day. As soon as the children enter your room on a rainy day, a science discussion begins. If the weather is unseasonably hot or cold, everyone cannot help but notice.

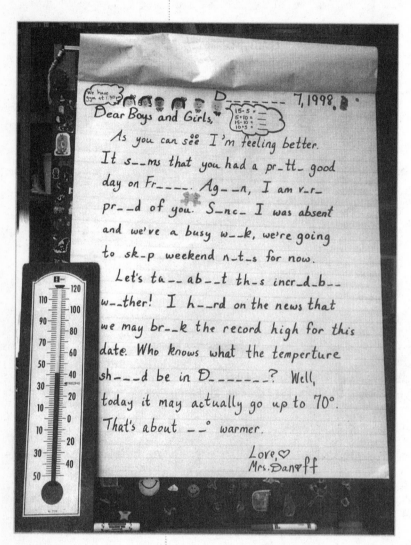

Integrating science is easy—just take a look out the window and write about the weather!

Taking Temperatures

During an unusual warm spell in New York in December of 1998, I wrote the letter at left to my first graders. Having a thermometer handy is always helpful, too.

Skill

✳ science discussion about temperature

Sample Lesson

Hannah: Mrs. Danoff, we're so glad you feel better. We missed you.

Mrs. Danoff: I'm glad I feel better too. Do you think this warm weather will help me feel even better?

Children: Yes!

Katie: Well, it's hard to get over a cold when it's cold. But my mom says the cold air kills more germs in the winter.

Mrs. Danoff: I've heard that too, Katie. So what should the temperature be in December?

Hannah: I think probably around 30 degrees so it can snow.

Mrs. Danoff: Oh Hannah, you're so right. What temperature does it have to be for snow?

Hannah: Freezing cold. It says freezing on that thermometer at about that, too.

Mrs. Danoff: Yes, and freezing is 32 degrees Fahrenheit or 0 degrees centigrade. What exactly is getting frozen when it snows?

Kyle: Rain!

Mrs. Danoff: Good for you! Just checking. So who can do the math? How much warmer is it today than it should be at this time of year? Should we add or subtract?

Kristina:	What can we subtract, from freezing?
Mrs. Danoff:	Good point, Kristina. Let's pick what we think would be the average temperature for December. Where could we find that information?
Jeffrey:	I saw that on the weather report this morning. The guy said it should have an average temperature of about 30 degrees in December. We could use that temperature.
Peter:	My mother has a Farmer's Almanac that she always checks. There are funny stories in there, too.
Mrs. Danoff:	So, okay everyone, should we go with 30 degrees as what it should be this time of year?
Children:	Yes!
Mrs. Danoff:	Then Alexandra, please move this thermometer down to 30 degrees. Okay, let's add up as Harpal moves the thermometer up to 70 degrees.
Children:	Ten, twenty, thirty, forty. Wow! It's going to be 40 degrees warmer today than it's supposed to be!
Katie:	Has that ever happened before?
Mrs. Danoff:	I remember it happening about ten years ago in December. There was a whole vacation week that was 60 degrees.

The discussions continues.

Extension Activities

❋ Use thermometers and cups of water to compare water temperatures.

❋ Hang a thermometer outside your classroom window and keep track of the temperatures for each month on class or individual charts.

Observing Our World

The letter dated May 26th discusses our science theme for the month: insects. The vocabulary associated with insects, like crawling and buzzing, easily work their way into a letter. The wonderful thing about this letter is that, in May, it was true. A mosquito woke me up, a spider was crawling along the counter, and there were ants everywhere!

I find that if I encourage students to observe their environment from the beginning of the school year, then they are ready to make accurate observations for our major science unit, which starts in April. The letters pictured on page 92 are examples of how to encourage children to observe what is around them, record the information, and draw conclusions.

This letter encourages students to observe and think about their environment.

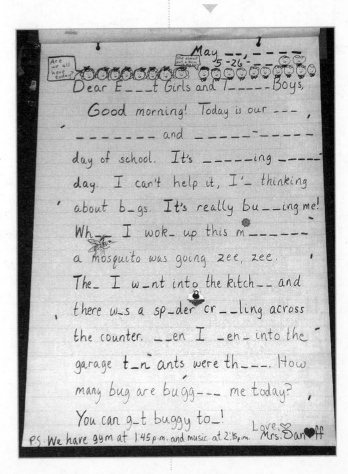

Ap___ 16, 19__

_ . _ . _ _

Dear T__ time S__ plus T__ time F___ Children,

Did any___ see all that fog this m_____g? I'd hea__ on the radio that it w____n't lift until midmorning. It _ertain_y seems to have disappeared. The sun is not out yet. So how could that have happen__? Is it the same thing that can cause the water level in our aqu__i___s to drop? If the water level drops by 2 cms, how far from the top will it be?

2.5cm. or 1"

Love
Mrs. Danoff

October 14, 1999

Dear Twelve plus Eight Children,
12 + 8 = 20 + 2 = 22

Gee, it's such a windy day! The wind is blowing from a northwest direction at about 30 miles per hour. Do you know what that means? How fast can you go? How fast can a car go? Anyone know how fast a squirrel can go?

I observed a squirrel for about five minutes yesterday. It was a grey squirrel. It scampered down a tree. Then quickly crossed the street. Next, it picked up an acorn in its front paws. The squirrel kind of looked at the acorn. Then scampered to another spot. It put the acorn down, dug a little hole and buried the acorn. Then it ran back across

---

Sharing my observations and wondering about them in daily letters like these helps students be more careful observers themselves.

Skill

✳ writing observations

Extension Activities

✳ Have the children go home and observe a squirrel or other animal for five minutes. As they do, they can write their observation in their writing journals.

✳ Have children keep individual or class science journals. For a class science journal, children can take turns being the recorder for observations and experiments.

Content-Area Vocabulary

Building vocabulary is an important piece of helping children understand science topics. Pictured here are two examples of how vocabulary can become a letter to your class.

The day before this lesson, the whole class had read the book, *What Food Is This?* by Rosmarie Hausherr, (Scholastic, 1995). It was full of rich vocabulary words. By the time we had finished reading the book, it was time to stop reading for the day. I knew we would pick up on the discussion the next day. After reading the November 4, 1999, letter, children supplied the list of words along the side of the letter from our previous day's reading. With real excitement we picked up the books again and checked the glossary and text for the meanings.

> *November 4, 1999*
>
> swamp
> wheat
> vegetarian
> stalk
> grain
> cluster
> homogenize
> pateurize
> artichoke
> harvest
> udder
> crop
> roughage
> nourish
> nutrient
> nutritious
> chlorophyll
>
> Dear Eleven times Two Children,   2392
> 11 × 2 = 22
>
> I had an interesting experience this morning. I was reading an article about shopping on the internet. The article said that companies can use the information they find out about you and give it to other companies. But, they only use it as an aggregate. I thought to myself, 'Wow! I know what that means!' I remembered the raspberry is an aggregate. So, for gathering data or information it must mean they group my information with other people's information to form a cluster. Like, a cluster of people that live in Westchester.
>
> Let's look at some more words we learned.
> slaughterhouse, cycle, steak, barbecue   Love, Mrs. Danoff

This letter demonstrates how easily science vocabulary can be woven into the Daily Letter.

> *May 5, 1999*
>
> Wacky!!   Can you find the spelling words?
>
> Dear Girls and Boys,
>
> How exciting! Our Are tanks will really become aquariums today. So far the aquariums have Elodea, Cabomba and gravel. One tank has a thermometer too. Today we can add the snails and guppies into to live with the plants. Before we do that we'll need to observe the vertebrates and mollusks. We can look for the snout and tentacles on the snails. We can look for the dorsal fin and gills on the guppies. Maybe, we'll even get too see how special a snail moves, because it's a gastropod. Oh, we'll also need to check the water level in our freshwater tanks.

Using the format of a Wacky Wednesday letter, I incorporated all the vocabulary words needed to introduce the study of fresh-water animals. Of course there was a great focus on some of the words, like Elodea and Cabomba. They looked like wacky misspelled words even though they were not.

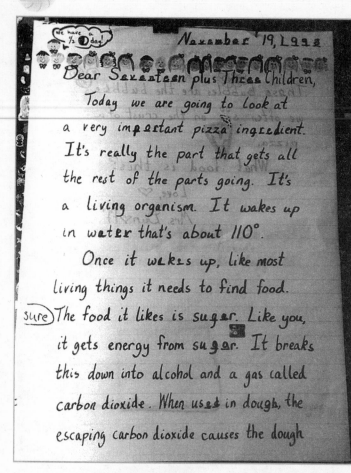

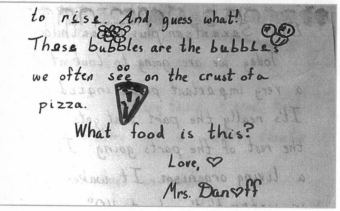

The Daily Letter is the perfect place to introduce a science experiment. Everything that is needed to complete the scientific process is spelled out right in front of the children, ready to discuss. Then, when the experiment is complete, the vocabulary is still there for the children to record and discuss again.

Integrating Social Studies and Science

Our food unit includes making pizza. Before we make it, the class studies all the ingredients that go into pizza. This study is also part of our farm-to-market study for social studies. The children learn about all the raw materials and the resources from which each ingredient is derived. However, asking the children what they know about pizza and what they want to know about pizza is where we begin. Inevitably, someone wants to know why pizza has bubbles in the crust. The yeast is the subject of this letter and an easily conducted experiment.

Extension Activity

For the yeast experiment you'll need five zip-lock bags, three packages of dry yeast, a teaspoon of sugar, a thermometer, and water heated to 110 degrees. Put the children into cooperative groups. Give each group a set of the above materials. In a zip-lock bag combine yeast with warm water and about one quarter teaspoon of sugar. Zip the bag closed. In about 10 minutes the bag will inflate from the gas being released. Have the children record the experiment.

Social studies and science topics surround us, and it's easy to incorporate them into the Daily Letter. I've found the Daily Letter to be an excellent forum for introducing and discussing all sorts of content-area topics.

CLOSING THOUGHTS

Dear Colleague,

I've always found letter writing a warm and friendly way to communicate with the children in my class. It's an ongoing dialogue that continues throughout the year. I can adapt the letter to suit the personality and needs of each class. From September to June, as we grow together, we learn together. And the Daily Letter reflects the honesty and love with which this happens. I wish the same for you!

REGARDS,

Valerie Schifferdanoff

Literature about Letters and Journals

Dear Peter Rabbit by Alma Flor Ada (Aladdin, 1994)

The Jolly Postman and Other People's Letters by Janet & Allan Ahlberg (William Heinemann Ltd. 1986)

My Worst Days Diary by Suzanne Altman (Byron P. Kreiss Visual Publications, 1995)

Your Best Friend Kate by Pat Brisson (Aladdin, 1992)

Learning to Swim in Swaziland: A Child's-eye View of a Southern African Country by Nila K. Leigh (Scholastic, 1993)

Night Letters by Palmyra LoMonaco (Dutton, 1996)

Flip's Fantastic Journal by Angelo DeCesare (Penguin, 1999)

Dear Mr. Blueberry by Simon James (Aladdin, 1991)

Euclid Bunny Delivers the Mail by Bruce Koscielniak (Alfred A. Knopf, 1991)

Rehema's Journey: A Visit in Tanzania by Barbara A. Margolies (Scholastic, 1990)

Amelia's Notebook by Marissa Moss (Tricycle Press, 1995)

The Long Long Letter by Elizabeth Spurr (Hyperion, 1997)

Thank You Santa by Margaret Wild (Omnibus Books, 1991)

The Magic Cornfield by Nancy Willard (Harcourt Brace, 1997)

Three Days on a River in a Red Canoe by Vera B. Williams (William Morrow & Co., 1981)